Meeting College Costs

What You Need to Know Before Your Child and Your Money Leave Home

MEETING COLLEGE COSTS

What You Need to Know Before Your Child and Your Money Leave Home

A Workbook for Families

The College Board
Educational Excellence for All Students

The College Board is a national nonprofit association that champions educational excellence for all students through the ongoing collaboration of more than 3,000 member schools, colleges, universities, education systems, and organizations. The Board promotes—by means of responsive forums, research, programs, and policy development—universal access to high standards of learning, equity of opportunity, and sufficient financial support so that every student is prepared for success in college and work.

Table of Contents

WHOSE OBLIGATION IS THIS, ANYWAY?

If you are like most parents who face the prospect of a child going off to college, you are excited about the opportunities that lie ahead—and filled with trepidation about how you will afford those opportunities and still have a life (not to mention a retirement) of your own. You have probably read about or heard about the cost of college today. And you are probably aware that for most families, providing a college education for their children is the largest investment (other than buying their home) that they will make.

Some families are convinced that they will get no help and will have to pay the total costs from current income and savings. Others believe that the costs of a college education should be shouldered by the government, the college, and the student. These families are neither completely right nor totally wrong.

THE FINANCING PARTNERSHIP

While it may be obvious that the student will benefit most from the college experience, others will benefit as well.

- You, the **parents,** will benefit through exposure to new ideas and the enjoyment from watching your child gain skills that lead to independence.

- The **country** will gain as your child moves into the world of work and becomes a taxpayer.

- **Employers** will gain another member of the trained workforce.

- **Colleges** will gain by increasing the group of loyal alumni who will support the institution in future years.

Just as buying your home involved a partnership—your investment, perhaps some family help, a mortgage lender—this major investment in a college education will likely involve a partnership as well. To some degree, unless you are extremely wealthy (and therefore probably not reading this book!), several of these partners may share in the financing of your child's education.

Most colleges will presume, however, that the primary responsibility for meeting college costs falls to parents. Over the months prior to your child's entering college, you will be asked to provide information about your financial circumstances so that federal and state governments, as well as the colleges to which your child is applying, can determine how much of the cost of education you will be able to pay. Your child's savings and income will also be taken into account. As you will learn later in this book, there are standardized methods of determining your family's expected share of the costs, but many colleges will try to be sensitive to your family's particular financial situation.

You will find that the other college financing partners offer a variety of options if college costs are beyond your financial ability.

- Your child may qualify for **grant money** (gift money that does not have to be repaid) from the federal government or your own state government, and/or from the college your child will attend. While some college-sponsored grants are awarded strictly on the basis of merit, most are offered based on financial need or a combination of need and merit.

➤ You and your child may also qualify for **low-interest loans** with favorable terms (for example, no payments due until after the student graduates from college).

➤ Some businesses and civic organizations offer **scholarship money** to students who meet their selection criteria.

➤ And there are increasing numbers of **opportunities** for families whose expected contribution *would* cover the cost of college **to borrow money** so that college payments can be spread over a longer time period.

HOW THIS BOOK CAN HELP

Meeting College Costs will give you the information you need to make the most of this partnership. You will learn:

➤ how to determine what the costs really are for each of the colleges your child is considering

➤ what types of financial aid are available

➤ how the government and the colleges will determine your eligibility for financial aid

➤ which financial aid forms to complete, and when

➤ how to interpret the financial aid offers your child receives

➤ what to do if the financial aid you receive is not enough

➤ why most families find that college is worth the cost

➤ how your high school–aged child fits into the college financing partnership

➤ how your child can manage his or her finances during college

You will find throughout the book special tips, charts and tables, case studies to which you can compare your own situation, and worksheets to help you make your way through the process as an informed consumer. We will also attempt to dispel some of the myths surrounding the financial aid process; and we'll provide definitions of the financial aid terms and acronyms most commonly used. Look for the following symbols in each chapter:

Important **tips** from the College Board

Myths—why commonly held beliefs aren't necessarily true

Additional **resources** for more information on a subject

Questions parents should ask colleges to become informed consumers

Helpful **worksheets** to help you prepare for the financial aid process

There are topics you won't find addressed in this book, such as the intricacies of rearranging one's financial situation in the effort to qualify for more aid, or details about the financial aid policies of particular colleges. We will, however, provide suggestions for other resources should you want more information.

Our first piece of advice? DON'T PANIC! By reading this book, you are on the way to understanding how you can send your child to a college that he or she will find compatible academically and socially, and that you as a family can afford.

Throughout the book you will find questions to ask the colleges to which your child is applying and worksheets to complete. If you do your homework, you'll be well-prepared to help your child make a good college choice.

How Much Will College REALLY Cost?

The first step in your planning process is to understand what the total costs will be at each of the colleges your child is considering. It might seem that defining costs should be relatively straightforward. In many cases, though, you will find that it is not. While information about "billable" costs (tuition, student fees, room and board) is readily available in each college's literature, you also need to be aware of other expenses that may have a substantial impact on total college costs.

Most colleges provide information for an average student's cost of attendance that includes tuition and student fees, room and board, as well as estimated expenses for books and supplies, personal expenses, and transportation to and from campus. Let's look at these components and some of the factors, hidden and otherwise, that could impact the total college cost.

7

COST COMPONENTS
Tuition

Tuition is one of the most easily defined components in the student budget. For most colleges there is a published cost for tuition per academic term. But some colleges link tuition to the number of credit hours the student takes, and other colleges charge tuition based on level of enrollment (part-time, full-time). In any case, it should be fairly easy to estimate annual tuition.

Consider strategies to reduce costs, such as shortening the time it takes to graduate by bringing in Advanced Placement credit or taking summer classes at a community college. Don't rule out a college solely on the basis of high tuition!

Fees

When fees are listed as a billable cost, they refer to the charges assessed every student to help pay for the necessary extras of campus life, usually in the student activity area. These fees help subsidize the cost of activities, such as concerts, lectures, and athletic events, so that most students will be able to attend events without large out-of-pocket expenses. The student activity fee is usually the same for everyone, and shouldn't require sleuthing to find out. Some fees that do require detective work are outlined below under "Other Costs."

Room and Board

There is variation in how colleges define room and board costs. Some have a set, billable cost for room and board, covering any room on campus and a one-size-fits-all meal plan. But others have a graduated scale of payment for housing, based on the assessed 'quality' of the living arrangement (single rooms often cost more, for example). You'll need to get a sense of the range of housing costs like these to put together a reasonable budget; the amount appearing in the cost-of-attendance budget is usually for the "average" room (in most cases a double in a typical residence hall). For schools offering meal plan options, be realistic about what your child will likely need; students who don't get up in time for breakfast should find a plan that covers only the other two meals of the day.

We can save a lot of money by having our child live at home during college.

While it is almost certain to cost less to have your child live at home rather than on campus, don't forget students who live at home cost money too! In addition to the food and utilities they consume at home, there will be the inevitable pick-up meals on campus. Among the big costs commuters must cover are car insurance and maintenance, gas, and parking fees, or the cost of public transportation. Unless it is essential to have your child live at home, be sure to consider the pluses of living on campus that are *not* quantifiable in terms of cost: more opportunities for your child to socialize and become involved in campus life and the opportunity to mature and become independent more quickly.

Books and Supplies

College viewbooks generally provide an estimate of what a typical student can expect to spend on books and supplies. Until your child is on campus and determines exactly which books and supplies are required in the courses he or she is taking, however, it is difficult to know where adjustments may need to be made in the estimate. Students majoring in English or history may find the estimate fairly accurate. Those majoring in biology or architecture may not.

It's best to find out what you can about variations in book expenses before enrollment, and plan to be economical if need be. A used book may be a better value than a new book, and at most colleges these are readily available.

Personal Expenses

As you might imagine, this is an area where the student's lifestyle can make a major difference in the cost. Colleges provide an estimate of what it is likely to cost a typical student to do laundry, go to campus events, order an occasional pizza, and the like. However, a penchant for late-night junk food, an insatiable need to see first-run movies, or a habit of long-distance calls to a friend can add up.

Transportation

It's essential to find out what a college considers in making an estimate of your child's travel expenses. For example, some residential colleges build into the total budget an allowance for two round-trips between home and college per year; others budget one or three. Depending on the distance home, car or air travel costs will be estimated. For colleges where students commute, some estimate will be made for commuting costs. You'll want to know what factors are considered in putting together the estimate (gas, parking, insurance, number of trips weekly) and determine as best you can how your child's actual experience may vary.

Other Costs

If all these costs weren't complicated enough, there are other, less obvious costs to consider.

- There may be special lab fees for some of the science courses your child plans to take, or drop-and-add fees for changing a course schedule.

- Many colleges charge students for health insurance. These fees may be waived on appeal. If your child has unusually high medical costs, consider those in making your plans.

- If your child is committed to decorating a residence hall room with posters, there may be a fee assessed at the end of the year to repair the walls.

- And, if your child decides to participate in such activities as athletics, music, or a sorority or fraternity, there will be additional costs.

You may well be able to find out about some of these costs in advance; if not, at least you know it would be advisable to plan on some miscellaneous additional costs beyond those addressed in the standard cost-of-attendance budget.

Keep track of the costs at the colleges your child is considering by completing the worksheet at the end of this chapter.

1997-98 ACADEMIC YEAR UNDERGRADUATE STUDENT BUDGETS

The following table displays average student charges and expenses for colleges responding to the College Board's most recent *Annual Survey of Colleges*. The sample budgets are illustrative of the kinds of fixed charges and additional expenses that students and their families will face during the 1997-98 academic year. (These costs will most likely increase for the next academic year.) "Resident" budgets represent expenses for students living on campus; "commuter" budgets illustrate costs that students who live at home will incur.

College Sector	Tuition and Fees	Books and Supplies	Room and Board	Transportation	Other Personal Expenses	Total Expenses
2-year public						
Commuter	$1,501	$610	$1,881	$978	$1,226	$6,196
2-year private						
Resident	6,855	617	4,543	610	1,072	13,697
Commuter	6,855	617	1,910	919	1,165	11,466
4-year public						
Resident	3,111	634	4,361	573	1,390	10,069
Commuter	3,111	634	1,963	960	1,465	8,133
4-year private						
Resident	13,664	631	5,549	537	1,043	21,424
Commuter	13,664	631	1,913	854	1,201	18,263

MEET THE SMITH, THE WASHINGTON, AND THE MARTINEZ FAMILIES

We will follow three representative students and their families as they move through the financial aid application and award and college selection processes. You may compare these families and their experiences to your own.

SARAH SMITH

Sarah expects to graduate near the top of her public high school class in June 1998 and major in English at college.

Sarah's parents are divorced. She lives with her mother, who is a secretary, and two younger brothers. The family rents an apartment in downtown Chicago.

Sarah's father is a teacher. As you'll see later, although her father no longer lives with the family, one of Sarah's college options will collect financial information from him and will expect him to help pay for her educational expenses.

Sarah is considering three colleges: Prairie (a four-year public university within commuting distance of home), Old Bricks (a four-year private college), and Central (another four-year private college). After some research, she and her mother determined the following costs for each:

	Prairie	Old Bricks	Central
Tuition and Fees	$3,250	$12,400	$9,500
Room and Board	(board only) 1,700	4,480	4,220
Books and Supplies	575	605	610
Personal Expenses	1,420	1,025	1,230
Transportation	890	525	700
TOTAL	$7,835	$19,035	$16,260

JAMES
WASHINGTON

James will graduate from a private preparatory school in Boston in June 1998. He is an above-average student and hopes to major in engineering at college.

James lives with both his parents. His father works in sales and his mother is an active volunteer in the community. James has a younger sister who also lives at home.

The family has unusually high medical expenses as a result of a long-term illness suffered by James's sister. The parents are buying their home.

James is considering three colleges: Colony (a four-year public university), Very Old Bricks (a four-year private college), and Division (another four-year private college located within commuting distance). James and his parents determined the following costs for each:

	Colony	Very Old Bricks	Division
Tuition and Fees	$4,300	$17,200	$12,800
Room and Board	4,730	6,520	(board only) 1,880
Books and Supplies	570	620	615
Personal Expenses	960	940	1,180
Transportation	420	440	850
TOTAL	$10,980	$25,720	$17,325

MARIA MARTINEZ

Maria grew up in Phoenix, Arizona, and will graduate from high school there in June 1998. A good student and a highly ranked tennis player, Maria plans to major in biology and pursue premedical studies in college.

Maria lives with her parents. Her mother is a dentist and her father is a real estate developer. The family includes six children: Maria, an older brother who is a college junior, and four younger children. The parents are homeowners.

Maria is also considering three colleges: Canyon (a two-year public college in Phoenix), Major Mortar (a four-year private college), and Midway (another four-year private college). Maria and her parents, after research, determined the following costs for each:

	Canyon	Major Mortar	Midway
Tuition & Fees	$ 835	$13,600	$11,100
Room and Board	(board only) 1,950	6,180	4,600
Books and Supplies	630	600	630
Personal Expenses	1,370	950	1,020
Transportation	740	400	700
TOTAL	$5,525	$21,730	$18,050

My child shouldn't even consider her first-choice college if it costs too much.

It's true that the total budgets for some colleges are lower than those for others. As you'll see when you fill in the College Costs worksheet at the end of this chapter, this is largely due to the difference in the cost of tuition. Tuition is subsidized at public colleges by taxpayers and is usually less at two-year public colleges than at four-year public colleges or universities. There's usually not a lot of difference in the other costs. You should also keep in mind that private colleges often have more financial aid, and more flexibility in awarding it, to help make up the difference between their costs and what your family can afford. As you'll see in Chapter 4, the greater your overall college expenses, the greater the possibility of demonstrating eligibility for financial aid.

For more information on college costs:

Admission and financial aid offices at colleges of interest

College and university Web sites on the Internet

College Board Online: *www.collegeboard.org.*

College Costs and Financial Aid Handbook, 1998. College Board Publications, 1997. This how-to reference for students and parents outlines major aid programs, discusses how financial aid is determined, and lists current costs and scholarship opportunities at 3,100 two- and four-year public, private, and proprietary institutions. Revised annually. Available in bookstores and in libraries.

ExPAN® This electronic college admission and guidance system, developed by the College Board, is available for use at participating high schools, colleges, and public libraries. The software allows you to research college costs at 3,100 colleges and universities and estimate how much your family will be asked to pay.

Chapter 2

Questions Families Should Ask About College Costs

You can find answers to these questions by reviewing college viewbooks and talking to admission and/or financial aid administrators at the colleges your child is considering.

1. Does the college charge a standard amount for tuition for the academic year, or does tuition vary by enrollment status (number of credits carried)? If tuition varies, what is the typical number of credits carried by first-year students? Upperclass students?

2. Does the college give academic credit for Advanced Placement courses? Under what conditions?

3. Does the cost of a dormitory room vary by the quality of the room? What is the cost of a single room? A double room? A triple room?

4. Are first-year students permitted to live off campus? What is the range of rental costs in the area of the campus?

5. Are there meal plan options? What meals are covered by the standard meal plan?

6. What are the typical costs for books and supplies for our child's intended major?

7. Are all students expected to own computers, or only students in certain majors? Are computers readily available in computer labs?

8. How much should we budget for our child's personal expenses? What types of expenses does this take into account?

9. Does the financial aid office take into account transportation home? How many round-trips per year? Is it assumed that our child will be flying or driving?

10. Are there special fees to consider?
    - lab fees?
    - health insurance? (Is this mandatory?)
    - music?
    - sorority/fraternity?
    - athletics?

WORKSHEET 1: COMPARING COLLEGE COSTS

College Name	1.	2.	3.	4.
Tuition				
Billable Fees				
Room Costs				
Board Costs				
Books/Supplies				
Personal Costs				
Transportation				
Other Costs				
TOTAL COSTS				

What Types of Financial Aid Are Available?

Now that you have a sense of the college costs you'll be facing, you are undoubtedly wondering where you might get help in meeting them. You'll find below a quick description of the major sources of financial aid available to families. Other private sources include:

➤ benefits offered by your employer

➤ competitive scholarships available from civic or religious groups

➤ scholarships targeted to students pursuing specific majors

If you'd like to know more about those types of opportunities, check with your child's guidance counselor, or follow up on some of the suggested resources at the end of the chapter.

Millions of scholarship dollars go unused every year.

If you're aware of this myth, you probably heard it from a representative of a scholarship search service. That's because they'd like you to pay them to look for these scholarships for you. The claim that millions go unused has never been verified. With the advice you're finding in this book, you should be able to find, without a professional search service, the money for which your child is eligible.

Three general categories of financial aid are awarded to undergraduate college students. Most students qualifying for aid will receive a combination of "gift" and "self-help" funding.

- **Grants and Scholarships** are funds awarded to students without expectation of repayment (sometimes referred to as "gift" aid). Sources of grants include federal and state governments, colleges, and private organizations.

- **Loans** are borrowed by students and parents to help meet college costs and must be repaid with interest. This "self-help" aid is available through the federal and state governments, institutions, and private lenders. The terms of some loans are more favorable than others, as you will see later in this chapter.

- **Student Employment.** The Federal Work-Study program is the best known of these "self-help" programs, where students work either on or off campus for an hourly salary. Some colleges have other student employment options either on or off campus.

FINANCIAL AID AVAILABLE THROUGH THE FEDERAL GOVERNMENT

The federal government is the largest single source of financial assistance for students and families. You and your child apply for this assistance by completing the Free Application for Federal Student Aid (FAFSA; you'll find more about that in Chapters 4 and 5).

Grants

Federal Pell Grants

This is the government's largest need-based student aid program. Pell Grants range from a minimum of $400 to a maximum of $3,000 for 1998-99. The size of the grant a student receives is based on the family's financial need, the cost of education at the college the student attends, the length of the program in which he or she is enrolled, and whether enrollment is full- or part-time.

Federal Supplemental Educational Opportunity Grants

Otherwise known as SEOG, these grants are campus-based, meaning that while the money comes from the federal government, the colleges are in charge of distributing the money to students who have financial need. Recipients must be enrolled in an undergraduate program at an accredited college or university. Grants of up to $4,000 a year are awarded on the basis of need.

Work-Study

Federal Work-Study Program (FWS)

This is a campus-based federal program providing employment opportunities for students who are enrolled at the undergraduate or graduate level. Students are usually employed on campus, though off-campus jobs can be arranged and are quite popular at some colleges. Students are generally paid at least the prevailing federal minimum wage. While students can work as many hours a week as their award will support, 10 to 15 hours is typical for first-year students. FWS eligibility is based on the student's demonstrated financial need.

Campus-Based Loans

Federal Perkins Loans

Perkins Loans are campus-based and administered by colleges and universities. They carry the lowest interest rate of any educational loans (5 percent) and repayment is deferred until a student graduates or leaves school. Students may be eligible to borrow up to $3,000 for each year of undergraduate study. Nine months after a student leaves school, regular payments are required over a maximum period of 10 years until the total amount, including interest, is repaid. Repayment can sometimes be further deferred for service in the military, the Peace Corps, or approved comparable organizations.

Federal Stafford Loan Program

Subsidized Federal Stafford Loans

These loans permit students with demonstrated need to borrow money for educational expenses from private sources (such as banks, credit unions, savings and loan associations, and educational organizations) at interest rates lower than most commercially available loans (though higher than Perkins Loans). The federal government pays the interest while the student is enrolled. Repayment is deferred until six months after a student graduates or leaves school.

Borrowers must be enrolled in college as at least half-time students. Freshmen may borrow up to $2,625 for the first year, and upperclassmen may borrow more, up to a maximum of $3,500 a year for dependent undergraduates who have completed their first year of study, and up to $5,500 a year for students who have completed two years of study. Under certain circumstances (at least half-time study, approved graduate fellowship programs, or economic hardship), repayment may be deferred temporarily. The repayment schedule is worked out between the student and the lender.

Unsubsidized Federal Stafford Loans

These loans are intended for use by students who do not qualify for a subsidized Stafford Loan and/or who need additional funds. The amounts, interest rates, and terms are generally the same as for the subsidized loans, with important differences: repayment begins as soon as the loan is disbursed; or, if the borrower opts to begin repayment after leaving school, he or she will be assessed interest charges from the time the loan is disbursed.

Federal Direct Student Loan Program (FDSLP)

Students at some postsecondary institutions can borrow subsidized and unsubsidized Federal Direct Loans through this program, which is administered at the college. If the college your child attends is participating in FDSLP, the financial aid office will tell you how to apply for these loans. The conditions are the same as outlined above.

Federal PLUS Loans

PLUS loans are available to parents of eligible students as an option for covering college costs. These loans are not need-based, but rather can be for any amount between the aid a student already has been awarded and the total cost of attendance. Parents must demonstrate creditworthiness to qualify for a PLUS Loan.

FINANCIAL AID AVAILABLE THROUGH STATES

Every state has a program to provide some form of need-based financial assistance to eligible students who are legal residents of the state. A few states also have funds available to students who meet specific eligibility requirements, regardless of need (for example, based on outstanding academic ability or program of study). Most of these aid funds are stipulated for use at colleges and universities within the state, although a few are "portable" (students can use the funds when attending a college in another state that has a reciprocal agreement with the home state). You'll want to check with your child's guidance counselor or the financial aid office at a local college, or contact your state education agency for information about what programs are available in your state and how to apply for them.

PRELIMINARY PROJECTED MONTHLY PAYMENT, FEDERAL STAFFORD PROGRAM

Amount Borrowed	Number of Payments	Estimated Monthly Payments*	Recommended Annual Salary
$ 2,625	66	$ 50	$ 7,500
$ 6,125	120	$ 75	$ 11,250
$ 11,625	120	$ 143	$ 21,450
$ 17,125	120	$ 210	$ 31,500
$ 23,000	120	$ 282	$ 42,300
$ 31,125	120	$ 382	$ 57,300
$ 39,625	120	$ 486	$ 72,900
$ 48,125	120	$ 590	$ 88,500
$ 56,625	120	$ 695	$ 104,250
$ 65,500	120	$ 803	$ 120,450

Recommended annual figures are based on 8 percent of income available for student loan repayment. Generally, manageable student loan payments range between 5 and 15 percent of income. Examples of average salaries follow on the next page.

* Minimum payment of $50.00. Interest rate of 8.25 percent.

ESTIMATED ANNUAL SALARIES

Listed below are the average annual salaries for a variety of careers. Keep in mind that these are averages, and many in each occupation earn more or less. For more information on salaries, please consult the latest edition of the *Occupational Outlook Handbook* at your library.

Up to $20,000

Cashier	$11,900	File Clerk	$16,200
Child Care Worker	13,520	Flight Attendant	15,700
Library Clerk	18,800	Hotel Desk Clerk	14,900
Data Entry Keyer	17,600	Nursing Aide	14,600
Dental Assistant	19,240	Receptionist	16,000

$20,000 to $29,000

Civil Engineer	$29,800	Graphics Designer	$25,600
Computer Operator	21,300	Personnel Clerk	25,100
Corrections Officer	22,900	Radio Announcer	27,900
Court Stenographer	20,700	Retail Jeweler	25,700
Financial Analyst	25,000	Travel Agent	21,300

$30,000 to $39,999

Bank Loan Officer	$36,400	Petroleum Engineer	$38,300
Data-Base Administrator	31,250	Public Relations Generalist	32,500
Computer-Aided Designer	30,700	Private Investigator	36,700
Executive Chef	37,000	Reference Librarian	35,600
Medical Scientist	36,300	Special Education Teacher	36,800
Newspaper Reporter	37,000	Stockbroker	37,300

$40,000 to $49,999

Affirmative Action Specialist	$42,500	Federal Contract Specialist	$47,900
Assistant Hotel Manager	40,000	Management Consultant	41,800
Chemist	45,400	Public School Counselor	42,500
Computer Systems Analyst	45,000	TV Sportscaster	48,700
Environmental Protection Analyst	49,170	Urban Planner	43,800

$50,000 to $74,999

Accounting Firm Partner	$70,100	High School Principal	$66,600
Air Traffic Controller	59,800	Internal Revenue Agent	50,700
Aviation Safety Inspector	62,900	Pharmacist	53,600
College Professor	63,500	Senior Newspaper Editor	60,000
Corporate Training Director	64,400	Software Engineer	53,500
FBI Agent	66,000	Veterinarian	56,500

$75,000 and Over

College President	$90,000	Optometrist	$80,000
Academic Dean of Business	78,600	Psychiatrist	120,000
Federal District Judge	133,600	Radiologist	240,000
Federal Patent Attorney	76,300	TV Anchorperson	200,000
Hospital CEO	165,600	U.S. Senator	134,000

Source: *Occupational Outlook Handbook.*

INSTITUTIONAL AID AVAILABLE THROUGH COLLEGES

Although the federal government may be the largest single source of financial assistance for families, a significant amount of aid comes from the colleges themselves. Private colleges offer a variety of forms of institutional aid; public colleges generally have fewer resources to make institution-based awards to students (but remember that taxpayer support makes tuition lower at these schools). Some colleges award grants ("scholarships" or "gift" aid are other terms they may use) solely on the basis of financial need. Others award grants on the basis of need and/or "merit" as determined by that institution. For example, there may be funds available to outstanding scholars, musicians, athletes, and the like.

Many campuses also have structured student employment programs to supplement the opportunities available through the Federal Work-Study program. These college-funded job programs may be based on student skills rather than student need, although some colleges do reserve these jobs exclusively for students with financial need.

Finally, college-sponsored long-term, short-term, and emergency loans are often available to all students. The best source of information about what institutional aid might be available is the financial aid office at each college your child is considering.

There's just not as much aid available as there used to be.

Perhaps when you went to college, you had all your higher education costs covered by outside sources. More likely, you didn't. Nonetheless, the myth persists that there simply is less money in "the system" to help pay for college these days. Actually, the reverse is true. To pick a recent 30-year period: in 1965, $600 *million* was available for financial aid. In 1995, $47 *billion* was available. As college costs have risen, so has the amount of money available to finance a college education. The kernel of truth in this myth is that the proportion of gift aid and self-help funding has shifted: loans and work make up a larger percentage of aid packages than they once did. That's why it's to your advantage to research as completely as possible the financing options available to your child at each of the colleges he or she is considering.

For more information about sources of financial aid:

Admission and financial aid offices at colleges of interest

College and university Web sites on the Internet

College Board Online: *www.collegeboard.org*

College Costs and Financial Aid Handbook, 1998

College Board Scholarship Handbook. The College Board, 1998. Lists more than 2,500 private and public scholarships, grants, loans, and internships covering more than 700,000 awards. Scholarships are indexed by majors/careers, ethnicity, gender, etc. Updated annually. Available in bookstores and in libraries.

ExPAN

High school guidance counselors

State scholarship/grant and loan programs

Questions Families Should Ask Colleges About
Financial Aid Funding Sources

1. Are admissions decisions at this college "need-blind" (financial status has no impact on decision), or "need-sensitive" (financial status can be a factor in admission decision)?

2. Does this college meet the full demonstrated need of admitted students?

3. Does the college offer institutionally funded gift aid? What percentage of freshman aid recipients receive such aid?

4. Are merit scholarships available? Are these awarded with or without regard to financial need?

5. Are there other special scholarships available that are awarded without regard to financial need?

6. What is the typical proportion of grant to loan in financial aid packages? Does the college give preferential aid packages (more grant, less loan) to some students? Which ones?

7. What is the typical number of hours per week that students must work to fulfill their work-study obligation?

8. Are work-study jobs readily available to financial aid recipients?

9. Are campus jobs available to students without regard to financial need?

10. Are college-sponsored, long-term loans available? Is financial need a criterion?

11. Are emergency loans available?

12. How are any outside scholarships that my child might be awarded treated in the awarding process? Do they reduce grant or self-help funding?

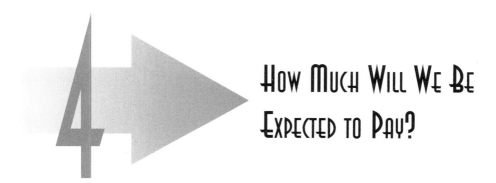

How Much Will We Be Expected to Pay?

Now that you are aware of the various financial aid sources that may be available to you to help meet college costs, you'll want to get a handle on how much you might be expected to pay. Most simply put, you and your child have the primary responsibility to pay and will be expected to contribute to the extent you are able.

Colleges use two standard formulas for determining how much your family will be expected to pay.

- **Federal Methodology (FM)**, based on the Free Application for Federal Student Aid (FAFSA) and used by the federal and state governments, and colleges, for awarding federal and state financial aid

- **Institutional Methodology (IM)**, based on the CSS/Financial Aid PRO-FILE® (a financial aid form produced by the College Scholarship Service®) and/or college-specific financial aid applications, and used by many colleges to award institutional funds

Financial aid administrators at the colleges to which your child is applying use their professional judgment along with the standard formulas to determine your eligibility for financial aid. You'll want to report your financial situation as completely and accurately as possible so that your expected family contribution reflects your family's circumstances.

DETERMINING THE EXPECTED FAMILY CONTRIBUTION
The Parents' Contribution

Income

Both Federal Methodology and Institutional Methodology base their calculations on the parents' total income for the calendar year prior to the one in which the student will enroll. Parents' wages and all other income (such as interest, dividends, social security, child support) are considered. Of course, not all of this income is available for college expenses, because much of it must be used for basic living expenses such as housing, food, medical care, clothing, and the like.

Aid administrators using IM also take into account other demands on your income, such as unusually high medical bills or, in some cases, unreimbursed tuition payments for children enrolled in elementary or secondary schools. After all these expenses are subtracted from income, a much smaller amount remains and is considered "available income," some of which you would be expected to use to pay college costs. In general terms, the more available income you have, the more you would be expected to contribute.

My income is too high; we'll never qualify for aid.

While income is certainly a key factor in determining whether a family qualifies for financial aid, it is not the only one. Your assets (or lack of assets), unusually high medical or other necessary expenses, the number of family members in college at the same time, private elementary or secondary school tuition payments, and other factors are often taken into account by college financial aid administrators. Many college students receiving aid come from families whose incomes are much higher than you might expect.

Assets

You'll find that aid formulas take assets into account as well, because families with assets are in a stronger financial situation than those without. All of your assets are added up: the value of a business, cash, savings and checking accounts, stocks and bonds, trust funds, and so forth. One of the major differences between Federal and Institutional Methodology is that IM also considers the equity in your home as an asset, while FM does not. IM also takes into account the equity in your farm; FM ignores this asset if the family lives on the farm.

Again, you will not be expected to use all your assets to pay for your child's education. The system protects a portion of assets for your retirement; the older you are, the more your retirement savings will be protected because you'll have less time in the future to save. The system also protects a substantial portion of assets you may have tied up in a business or farm, because they are sources of future income. Even after any allowances are deducted, you won't be expected to use all the remaining assets for educational costs but only a small portion, usually about 3 to 6 percent of the total amount.

I'll have to sell my house to pay for college.

Although many colleges will consider your home equity in determining how much you will be expected to pay, they will not expect you to sell your home. The larger portion of what your family will be expected to pay will come from your income, not your assets. At a maximum, 6 percent of the value of parents' assets (including home equity, savings, stocks and bonds, and the like) will be considered "available" to help meet college costs. You may find that you can tap into the equity in your home by borrowing against it to help finance your expected contribution, and you may receive an added benefit of deducting payments on your federal income tax return. And remember, home value is not even considered in determining eligibility for the federal student aid programs.

Multiple Family Members in College

Both the Federal and Institutional Methodologies take into account the number of family members enrolled in college. In other words, the amount you are considered to have available from income and assets is divided by the number of family members enrolled in college at least half time. It is important to keep this in mind, especially if you don't qualify for aid when your oldest child goes to college; you may well be eligible for assistance once the younger ones do.

Unlike the FM procedure, Institutional Methodology does not include parents in the number-in-college adjustment. The IM treatment acknowledges that many parents enrolled in college attend less than half time or have their costs covered by employer educational benefit programs.

Some colleges take into account the relative costs of the colleges attended by the applicant's siblings and do not divide the contribution equally among the children. Rather, they apportion the contribution. For example, if the applicant's sister is attending a low-cost community college, a higher-cost private college will expect that most of the computed contribution will be available to the student at the high-cost school.

Divorced Parents

Both Federal Methodology and Institutional Methodology take into account only the financial situation of the biological parent with whom the child has spent the greatest amount of time in the calendar year prior to college enrollment. (If that parent has remarried, the stepparent's financial information is also considered.) However, some colleges request information from the non-custodial parent and take that parent's financial situation into account in determining the expected family contribution. These schools adhere to the principle that both parents, regardless of their current marital status, have the primary responsibility for providing for their child's education and should be expected to provide reasonable financial support before college resources are used.

Federal Methodology Variations

The FM provides two formula variations, depending on the level of parent taxable income and federal tax (IRS) filing status. For parents and students who file or are eligible to file IRS 1040A or 1040EZ forms, or who aren't required to file income tax forms, no assets are included in the FM calculation if the parents' taxable income is less than $50,000. In instances where parents file or are eligible to file 1040A or 1040EZ forms, or aren't required to file income tax forms, and have taxable income of $12,000 or less, the FM Expected Family Contribution is automatically reduced to zero. (The Institutional Methodology has no such variations. Its formula is applied consistently, regardless of family income and asset levels.)

The Student's Contribution

Income and Assets

Your child's income for the previous year, as well as his or her assets (generally savings or investments held in your child's name) will be considered in a similar manner to yours. Because your child is the member of the college financing partnership who will benefit most directly, he or she will be expected to contribute a higher percentage of income and assets to meet college costs than you will. Students generally are expected to contribute about 50 percent of their available income and 35 percent of their assets each year toward meeting college costs.

The Federal and Institutional Methodologies differ in their expectations of the student contribution from income. Under FM, students earning up to $1,750 (including income from assets) during the calendar year prior to enrollment are not expected to make any contribution from income. Under IM, the student's contribution is expected to be at least $1,050 (higher at some colleges).

Independent or Dependent?

If your child is considered independent of you for financial aid consideration, your finances will not be taken into account in determining the federal family contribution. (Some institutions, for purposes of awarding their institutional aid, may require parent information, regardless of the student's dependency status.) To be considered independent for federal financial aid purposes, your child must answer "yes" to at least one of these six questions:

- Is the student 24 or older?

- Is the student married?

- Is the student enrolled in a graduate or professional school program?

- Does the student have dependents other than a spouse?

- Is the student an orphan or ward of the court?

- Is the student a military veteran?

The FM and IM formulas treat independent students differently from students who are dependent on their parents. The case studies in this book illustrate dependent student circumstances. However, worksheets for independent student calculations are included at the end of the chapter.

ELIGIBILITY FOR AID

In general, you are considered eligible for aid if there is a difference between the cost of attendance at the colleges your child is considering (see Chapter 3) and your expected family contribution. This difference is referred to as your "demonstrated financial need." The specific aid for which you will qualify varies by the source.

We shouldn't have saved for college—our child would have qualified for more aid.

This statement only makes sense if you would prefer college costs to take a bigger bite out of your current income and if you would prefer your child to begin his or her career with higher college loan payments due. Families with substantial demonstrated need will certainly find that they qualify for more aid, and it is comforting to know that there is a system in place to help families meet college costs. But families that have saved for college will have greater flexibility: there won't be as much concern about where to apply based on how much aid might be available, and the family's lifestyle may not be significantly altered. And, for families that begin saving for college while their children are still young, a relatively modest monthly savings account for college will grow dramatically by the time the college years arrive. So be glad you saved for college—you'll probably enjoy your child's college years more than families that didn't save!

Federal Aid

Federal Pell Grants

Eligibility is determined by your federal expected family contribution. The size of the grant is based on a table produced annually by the U.S. Department of Education. Students with lower estimated family contributions receive larger grants.

Federal SEOG

Eligibility is determined at the campus level. SEOG is intended to enhance educational opportunity for low-income students or help students with a high demonstrated need. Most colleges limit SEOG eligibility to those students who also qualify for a Federal Pell Grant.

Federal Work-Study (FWS)

Eligibility is based on demonstrated need. The determination to award FWS is made at the campus level.

Federal Perkins Loans

Eligibility is determined at the college level, with the government stipulation that these loans should go to students with "exceptional need" as defined by the college.

Subsidized Loans

Your child is eligible for a Federal Stafford Loan or a Federal Direct Student Loan if you have demonstrated need based on the Federal Methodology.

Unsubsidized Loans

Your child may be eligible for an unsubsidized Federal Stafford or Direct Loan regardless of whether your family demonstrates need; if you make the determination that aid from other sources is not enough to cover the cost of attendance, you may apply for these loans.

PLUS Loans

As a parent you are eligible to borrow any sum of money through the PLUS program up to the cost of attendance minus any other aid received. Your family does not have to demonstrate financial need to qualify.

State Aid

State Scholarships and Grants

Eligibility is determined by each state program, and there is some variation from one state to another. In most states, need-based scholarships and grants are awarded on the basis of the number of eligible applicants, the amount of money supporting the program, and a ranking of applicant need determined by the state's use of FM or a variation of that formula. A student's academic record and/or scores on standardized admission tests, such as the SAT® or ACT, may also be considered in the awarding of some competitive state scholarships. State scholarships and grants are limited to qualified state residents.

State Loans

Some states have student or parent loan programs in addition to the federal loan programs described above. Check with your state financial aid agency or college financial aid offices to learn about any state-funded loan program that might be available to you.

Institutional Aid

As you may have noticed, college financial aid administrators have some flexibility even in the awarding of federal aid to students. They have much greater latitude in awarding their own institution-sponsored aid.

You already know that many colleges use the Institutional Methodology and require that the PROFILE or other additional financial aid applications be completed, in addition to the FAFSA, so that they can gain a clearer picture of your family's financial situation. But you should also be aware that several colleges can look at the same family's information and IM results and come up with different expected family contributions and thus different figures for demonstrated financial need. As we follow up with our case studies, you will see examples of differing determinations by colleges.

What's important to keep in mind here is that institutions, not formulas, determine how institutional funds will be awarded. To plan well, it will be important for you to find out as much as you can about each college's policies for assessing the family contribution and determining eligibility for financial aid.

My child isn't an "A" student; we'll never get aid.

While there are a significant number of merit scholarships that recognize academic talent and reward students regardless of their financial circumstances, by far the majority of financial aid awarded these days goes to students with demonstrated financial need. If your child is admitted to a college that awards most financial aid on the basis of demonstrated need, straight A's will not be the key factor in determining the amount of the award.

EXPECTED FAMILY CONTRIBUTION AND DEMONSTRATED NEED

You can use the worksheets at the end of this chapter to estimate your family's expected contribution. The following calculations of expected contributions are for the students and families you met in Chapter 2.

SARAH SMITH

All the colleges in which Sarah is interested use only the Federal Methodology to determine eligibility for financial aid. Sarah's mother earned $25,070 in wages in 1997 and an additional $800 in taxable income (interest and dividends). She also received $12,000 in child support, which was untaxed. **The total family income was $37,870**.

From this total income figure, FM allows deductions for U.S. income tax, state and other taxes, and social security taxes (totaling $5,869 in Sarah's mother's case). In addition, allowances are made for employment expenses and basic living expenses (another $21,310). Altogether, $27,179 in allowances is deducted from the total family income to arrive at **$10,691 in available income**.

As for assets, Sarah's mother has $2,500 in savings and $15,000 in investment equity. From the total of these assets, no contribution would be expected because the family qualifies for the "simple needs test" (see FM variations on page 33). **The adjusted available income remains at $10,691.** From this, **$2,352 would be the expected parent contribution.**

As for Sarah's contribution, FM takes into account the $1,500 she earned in wages in 1997. After taking allowances for state and other taxes and income protection, Sarah's available income is -$425; she will not be expected to make any contribution from income. While she does have $300 in a savings account, the fact that her family qualifies for the "simple needs test" means Sarah would not be expected to make a contribution from assets.

Thus, **the total expected family contribution, under Federal Methodology, would be $2,352.**

Parents' expected contribution: Sarah Smith	Federal Methodology
A. 1997 income	
1. Father's yearly wages, salary, tips, and other compensation	$0
2. Mother's yearly wages, salary, tips, and other compensation	$25,070
3. All other income of mother and father (dividends, social security, pensions, welfare, child support, etc.)	$12,800
4. IRS allowable adjustments to income (business expenses, interest penalties, alimony paid, etc.)	$0
B. Total income	$37,870
C. Total allowances against income	$27,179
D. Available income	$10,691
E. Assets	
1. Cash, savings, and checking accounts	$2,500
2. Other investments (current net value)	$15,000
F. Total assets	$17,500
G. Asset protection allowance	$0
H. Remaining assets	$0
I. Income supplement from assets	$0
J. Adjusted available income	$10,691
K. **Parents' expected contribution**	**$2,352**

JAMES WASHINGTON

One of James's college choices relies on the Institutional Methodology to award institutional aid. (The other two choices use the FM.) James's father earned $65,300 in salary in 1997; his parents also earned $500 in interest on investments. They received $2,000 in untaxed benefits. Thus, **the total family income was $67,800**.

From this total figure, both Federal Methodology and Institutional Methodology allow deductions for U.S. income tax, state and other taxes, social security taxes, and basic living expenses. In addition to these allowances, IM provides an allowance for the heavy medical expenses James's family incurred. This consideration results in the difference between the FM allowances (totaling $36,074) and IM allowances (totaling $40,434). This difference is reflected in the two **available income** figures in the following table: **$31,726 for FM** and **$27,366 for IM**.

As for assets, James's parents have $800 in savings and $7,500 in investment equity. They also have $20,300 in home equity, which is taken into consideration by Institutional Methodology but not by Federal Methodology. For **FM** purposes, James's family has **$8,300 in total assets**; for **IM** purposes, the **asset total is $28,600**. From these assets, both methodologies allow for asset protection for retirement that is greater than the total assets; thus, no contribution would be expected from these assets and the **adjusted available income** remains the same: **$31,726 for FM and $27,366 for IM**. James's parents would be expected to contribute **$10,578 under FM and only $8,529 under IM**.

As for James's contribution, both methodologies take into account the $2,850 he earned in wages in 1997 and his $50 income from investments. After taking allowances for state and other taxes and income protection, James's available income is $845 (FM), with his expected contribution from income figured at $423 (FM). Under Institutional Methodology, no income protection is provided: after taking allowances, IM considers James's available income to be $2,435, of which $1,218 would be expected as his contribution from income. James also has $1,000 in savings. From this, $350 would be expected under both FM and IM. Thus, James's **total expected student contribution would be $773 (FM) and $1,568 (IM)**.

Adding the totals for parent and student contributions, James's **expected family contribution under FM would be $11,351; and under IM, $10,097**.

Parents' expected contribution: James Washington	FM	IM
A. 1997 income		
1. Father's yearly wages, salary, tips, and other compensation	$65,300	$65,300
2. Mother's yearly wages, salary, tips, and other compensation	$0	$0
3. All other income of mother and father (dividends, social security, pensions, welfare, child support, etc.)	$2,500	$2,500
4. IRS allowable adjustments to income (business expenses, interest penalties, alimony paid, etc.)	$0	$0
B. Total income	$67,800	$67,800
C. Total allowances against income	$36,074	$40,434
D. Available income	$31,726	$27,366
E. Assets		
1. Cash, savings, and checking accounts	$800	$800
2. Other investments (current net value)	$7,500	$7,500
3. Home equity		$20,300
F. Total assets	$8,300	$28,600
G. Asset protection allowance	$38,200	$36,500
H. Remaining assets	-$29,900	-$7,900
I. Income supplement from assets	$0	$0
J. Adjusted available income	$31,726	$27,366
K. **Parents' expected contribution**	**$10,578**	**$8,529**

MARIA MARTINEZ

Both of the private colleges in which Maria is interested use the IM to determine eligibility for institutional funds. The public college uses the FM. Maria's father earned $70,500 in salary in 1997; her mother earned $79,000. In addition, her parents earned $5,650 in interest on investments. Thus, the **total family income was $155,150.**

From this total figure, both Federal Methodology and Institutional Methodology allow deductions for U.S. income tax, state and other taxes, social security taxes, and basic living expenses. In addition to these allowances, IM provides an allowance for the medical expenses Maria's large family incurred. This consideration results in the difference between the FM allowances (totaling $82,938) and IM allowances (totaling $88,552). This difference is reflected in the two **available income** figures in the following table: **$72,212 for FM** and **$66,598 for IM.**

As for assets, Maria's parents have $4,800 in savings and $90,000 in investment equity. They also have $75,500 in home equity, which is taken into consideration by Institutional Methodology but not by Federal Methodology. For **FM** purposes, Maria's family has **$94,800 in total assets**; for **IM** purposes, the **asset total is $170,300**. From these assets, both methodologies allow for protection for retirement that is *less* than the total assets. The **adjusted available income** including the supplement from available assets is **$77,984 for FM and $81,250 for IM**. Taking into account that Maria's brother is attending college full time, **$16,160 would be expected as the FM contribution**; $16,928 as the expected parent contribution under IM.

As for Maria's contribution, both methodologies take into account the $600 she earned in wages in 1997 and her $30 income from investments. After taking allowances for state and other taxes and income protection, Maria's available income is $0 (FM). Under Institutional Methodology, no income protection is provided: after taking allowances, IM considers Maria's available income to be $578. Since IM sets a minimum of $1,050 as the student contribution, $1,050 would be expected as Maria's contribution from income, based on a combination of 1997 and assumed 1998 earnings. Maria also has $500 in savings. From this, $175 would be expected under both FM and IM. Thus, Maria's **total expected student contribution would be $175 (FM) and $1,225 under IM**.

Adding the totals for parent and student contributions, Maria's **expected family contribution under FM would be $16,335; and under IM, $18,153**.

Parents' expected contribution: Maria Martinez	FM	IM
A. 1997 income		
1. Father's yearly wages, salary, tips, and other compensation	$70,500	$70,500
2. Mother's yearly wages, salary, tips, and other compensation	$79,000	$79,000
3. All other income of mother and father (dividends, social security, pensions, welfare, child support, etc.)	$5,650	$5,650
4. IRS allowable adjustments to income (business expenses, interest penalties, alimony paid, etc.)	$0	$0
B. Total income	$155,150	$155,150
C. Total allowances against income	$82,938	$88,552
D. Available income	$72,212	$66,598
E. Assets		
1. Cash, savings, and checking accounts	$4,800	$4,800
2. Other investments (current net value)	$90,000	$90,000
3. Home equity		$75,500
F. Total assets	$94,800	$170,300
G. Asset protection allowance	$46,700	$48,200
H. Remaining assets	$48,100	$122,100
I. Income supplement from assets	$5,772	$14,652
J. Adjusted available income	$77,984	$81,250
K. Parents' expected contribution	$32,319	$33,855
L. **Parents' contribution if 2 family members in college**	**$16,160**	**$16,928**

 For more information on calculating family contributions:

College and university Web sites

College Board Online: *www.collegeboard.org*

College Costs and Financial Aid Handbook, 1998

Financial aid offices at colleges of interest

Questions Families Should Ask About How Their Expected
Contribution Will Be Determined

The following questions relate to how each of the colleges your child is considering will determine your expected contribution toward that college's costs, and thus your demonstrated need, if any, for college-sponsored funds. You'll be able to get answers to these questions from financial aid administrators at your child's college choices.

1. What methodology or formula does this college use in determining financial need for college-sponsored aid programs?

2. If the college uses an Institutional Methodology, what college-specific adjustments are made, if any?

3. Does the college consider the noncustodial parent's income and assets? If so, does the college also consider the stepparent's income and assets?

4. What is the minimum student contribution expected by the college?

5. Does the college consider medical or dental expenses?

6. Does the college make an allowance for elementary or secondary school tuition costs for younger children in the family?

7. What is the college's policy about treatment of business or farm assets?

8. Does the college consider home assets? If so, how?

9. Does the college consider costs of the parent's college enrollment?

10. How does the college adjust the contribution to account for the costs of the sibling's college enrollment?

WORKSHEET 2: ESTIMATING ELIGIBILITY USING FEDERAL METHODOLOGY

Refer to the tables on pages 48 and 49 to complete this worksheet.

WORKSHEET 2: Parents

PARENTS' INCOME	
1. AGI/taxable income	$
2. Total untaxed income/benefits	+
3. Child support paid	−
4. Total parents' income (sum of lines 1 and 2, minus line 3)	=
ALLOWANCES	
5. U.S. income tax	
6. State and other taxes (% from Table 1 times line 4)	+
7. F.I.C.A. (Table 2)	+
8. Income Protection Allowance (Table 3a)	+
9. Employment allowance (Table 2)	+
10. Total Allowances (sum of lines 5, 6, 7, 8, and 9)	=
11. Available Income (line 4 minus line 10)	
PARENTS' ASSETS	
12. Cash, savings, and checking accounts	
13. Other real estate/investment equity	+
14. Adjusted business/nonfamily farm equity (Table 4)	+
15. Net worth (sum of lines 12 to 14)	=
16. Asset Protection Allowance (Table 5)	−
17. Discretionary net worth (line 15 minus line 16)	=
18. Conversion percentage	× 12%
19. Income Supplement (line 17 × line 18) **(If Simple Needs Test qualifier*, enter $0; if negative, enter $0)**	=
20. Adjusted available income (sum of lines 11 and 19)	
CONTRIBUTION**	
21. Total contribution (calculate using line 20 and Table 8)	=
22. Number of family members enrolled in college at least half time	÷
23. Parents' contribution for student (line 21 divided by line 22); can't be less than 0	=

* For parents and students who file or are eligible to file IRS 1040A or EZ forms or who aren't required to file, no assets are included in the methodology if parents' taxable income is less than $50,000.

** Federal need analysis provisions provide a 0 EFC variant for families with parents' AGI of $12,000 or less. The parents must file or be eligible to file the 1040A or 1040EZ federal income tax return, or do not file taxes. In such cases, no contribution would be expected.

WORKSHEET 2 *continued*: Dependent Student

STUDENT'S INCOME	
1. AGI/taxable income	$
2. Untaxed income/benefits	+
3. Taxable student aid	–
4. Total income (sum of lines 1 and 2, minus line 3)	=
ALLOWANCES	
5. U.S. income tax	
6. State and other taxes (% from Table 1 times line 4)	+
7. F.I.C.A. (Table 2)	+
8. Income Protection Allowance	+ $1,750
9. Total Allowances (sum of lines 5, 6, 7, and 8)	=
10. Available Income (line 4 minus line 9)	=
11. Contribution from income (line 10 × 50%); cannot be less than $0	=
STUDENT'S ASSETS	
12. Cash, savings, and checking accounts	
13. Other real estate/investment equity	+
14. Business/nonfamily farm equity	+
15. Net assets (sum of lines 12 to 14)	=
16. Contribution from assets (line 15 times .35); cannot be less than $0 (If Simple Needs Test qualifier*, enter $0)	=
CONTRIBUTION**	
17. TOTAL STUDENT'S CONTRIBUTION (Sum of lines 11 and 16)	=

* For parents and students who file or are eligible to file an IRS 1040A or EZ form or who aren't required to file, no assets are included in the methodology if parents' taxable income is less than $50,000.

** Federal need analysis provisions provide a 0 EFC variant for families with parents' AGI of $12,000 or less. The parents must file or be eligible to file the 1040A or 1040EZ federal income tax return, or do not file taxes. In such cases, no contribution would be expected.

WORKSHEET 2 *continued*: Independent student with dependents (other than a spouse)

STUDENT'S (AND SPOUSE'S) INCOME	
1. AGI/taxable income	$
2. Total untaxed income/benefits	+
3. Income exclusions (child support paid + taxable student aid)	−
4. Total income (sum of lines 1 and 2, minus line 3)	=
ALLOWANCES	
5. U.S. income tax	−
6. State and other taxes (% from Table 1 times line 4)	−
7. F.I.C.A. (Table 2)	−
8. Income Protection Allowance (Table 3a)	
9. Employment allowance (Table 2)	+
10. Total Allowances (sum of lines 5, 6, 7, 8, and 9)	=
11. Available Income (line 4 minus line 10)	
STUDENT'S (AND SPOUSE'S) ASSETS	
12. Cash, savings, and checking accounts	
13. Other real estate/investment equity	+
14. Adjusted business/nonfamily farm equity (Table 4)	+
15. Net worth (sum of lines 12 to 14)	=
16. Asset Protection Allowance (Table 5)	−
17. Discretionary net worth (line 15 minus line 16)	=
18. Conversion percentage	× 12%
19. Income Supplement (line 17 × line 18) **(If Simple Needs Test qualifier*, enter $0; If negative, enter $0)**	=
20. Adjusted available income (sum of lines 11 and 19)	=
CONTRIBUTION**	
21. Total contribution (calculate using line 20 and Table 8)	=
22. Number of family members in college enrolled at least half time	÷
23. Contribution for student	=

* For students who file or are eligible to file IRS 1040A or EZ forms or who aren't required to file, no
  assets are included in the methodology if student's taxable income is less than $50,000.
** Federal need analysis provisions provide a 0 EFC variant for families with student's AGI of $12,000 or less. The
  student must file or be eligible to file the 1040A or 1040EZ federal income tax return, or does not file taxes.
  In such cases, no contribution would be expected.

WORKSHEET 2 *continued*: Independent student without dependents (other than a spouse)

STUDENT'S (AND SPOUSE'S) INCOME	
1. AGI/taxable income	$
2. Total untaxed income/benefits	+
3. Income exclusions (child support paid + taxable student aid)	–
4. Total income (sum of lines 1 and 2, minus line 3)	=
ALLOWANCES	
5. U.S. income tax	
6. State and other taxes (% from Table 1 × line 4)	+
7. F.I.C.A. (Table 2)	+
8. Employment allowance (Table 2)	+
9. Income Protection Allowance (Table 3b)	+
10. Total Allowances (sum of lines 5, 6, 7, 8, and 9)	=
11. Available Income (line 4 minus line 10)	
12. Student's contribution from income (line 11 × 50%)	=
STUDENT'S (AND SPOUSE'S) ASSETS	
13. Cash, savings, and checking accounts	
14. Other real estate/investment equity	+
15. Adjusted business/nonfamily farm equity (Table 4)	+
16. Net worth (sum of lines 13 to 15)	=
17. Asset Protection Allowance (Table 5)	
18. Discretionary net worth (line 16 minus line 17)	=
19. Student's contribution from assets (line 18 times .35) **(If Simple Needs Test qualifier*, enter $0; cannot be less than $0)**	=
CONTRIBUTION	
20. TOTAL STUDENT'S CONTRIBUTION (Sum of lines 12 and 19, divided by 2 if spouse is enrolled)	=

* For students who file or are eligible to file IRS 1040A or EZ forms or who aren't required to file, no assets are included in the methodology if students' taxable income is less than $50,000.

1998-99 CSS
Federal Methodology (FM)
Computation Tables

TABLE 1. ALLOWANCES FOR STATE AND OTHER TAXES

State/Territory/Country of Residence	Parents of Dependent Students and Independent Students with Dependents		Dependent and Independent w/ NO Dependents
	Total Income		Total Income
	$ 0- 15,000	$15,001 or more	Any amount
Alabama (AL)	5 %	4 %	3 %
Alaska (AK)	3	2	0
American Samoa (AS)	4	3	2
Arizona (AZ)	6	5	3
Arkansas (AR)	6	5	4
California (CA)	8	7	5
Canada (CN)	4	3	2
Colorado (CO)	7	6	4
Connecticut (CT)	6	5	2
Delaware (DE)	8	7	5
District of Columbia (DC)	10	9	7
Federated States of Micronesia (FM)	4	3	2
Florida (FL)	4	3	1
Georgia (GA)	7	6	4
Guam (GU)	4	3	2
Hawaii (HI)	8	7	6
Idaho (ID)	7	6	5
Illinois (IL)	6	5	2
Indiana (IN)	6	5	4
Iowa (IA)	8	7	5
Kansas (KS)	7	6	4
Kentucky (KY)	7	6	5
Louisiana (LA)	4	3	2
Maine (ME)	9	8	5
Marshall Islands (MH)	4	3	2
Maryland (MD)	9	8	6
Massachusetts (MA)	9	8	5
Mexico (MX)	4	3	2
Michigan (MI)	9	8	4
Minnesota (MN)	9	8	6
Mississippi (MS)	5	4	3
Missouri (MO)	6	5	3
Montana (MT)	8	7	5
Nebraska (NE)	8	7	4
Nevada (NV)	3	2	0
New Hampshire (NH)	7	6	1
New Jersey (NJ)	8	7	3
New Mexico (NM)	6	5	4
New York (NY)	11	10	7
North Carolina (NC)	8	7	5
North Dakota (ND)	6	5	2
Northern Mariana Islands (MP)	4	3	2
Ohio (OH)	8	7	5
Oklahoma (OK)	6	5	4
Oregon (OR)	10	9	6
Palau (PW)	4	3	2
Pennsylvania (PA)	7	6	3
Puerto Rico (PR)	4	3	2
Rhode Island (RI)	9	8	4
South Carolina (SC)	8	7	5
South Dakota (SD)	4	3	0
Tennessee (TN)	3	2	0

TABLE 1., continued

State/Territory/Country of Residence	Parents of Dependent Students and Independent Students with Dependents		Dependent and Independent w/ NO Dependents
	Total Income		Total Income
	$ 0- 15,000	$15,001 or more	Any amount
Texas (TX)	3 %	2 %	0 %
Utah (UT)	8	7	5
Vermont (VT)	8	7	4
Virgin Islands (VI)	4	3	2
Virginia (VA)	8	7	4
Washington (WA)	4	3	0
West Virginia (WV)	6	5	4
Wisconsin (WI)	10	9	5
Wyoming (WY)	3	2	0
Not Reported (NR)	4	3	2

TABLE 2. ALLOWANCES AGAINST INCOME

FICA: *Wages*

$1 to 65,400 ... 7.65% of income earned by each wage earner (maximum $5,003.10 per person)

$65,401 or more ... $5,003.10 + 1.45% of income earned above $65,400 by each wage earner

Employment allowance ... 35% of lesser earned income to maximum $2,800 (single parent: 35% of earned income to maximum of $2,800)

TABLE 3a. INCOME PROTECTION ALLOWANCE (IPA)
(Parents of Dependent Students/Independent Students with Dependents)

Family Size* including student	Number in College**				
	1	2	3	4	5
2	$12,030	$9,980			
3	14,990	12,940	$10,880		
4	18,510	16,450	14,400	$12,340	
5	21,840	19,780	17,730	15,670	$13,630
6	25,550	23,490	21,440	19,380	17,330

* For each additional family member, add $2,880.
**For each additional college student, subtract $2,050.

TABLE 3b. INCOME PROTECTION ALLOWANCE
(Dependent Students and Independent Students with NO Dependents)

Dependent Student ... $1,750

Single Independent ... 3,000

Married Independent (student and spouse enrolled) ... 3,000

Married Independent (only student is enrolled) ... 6,000

1998-99 CSS
Federal Methodology (FM)
Computation Tables

TABLE 4. ADJUSTED NET WORTH OF A BUSINESS OR FARM

Net Worth (NW)	Adjusted Net Worth
Less than $1	$ 0
$ 1 to 85,000	$ 0 + 40% of NW
$ 85,001 to 255,000	$ 34,000 + 50% of NW over $ 85,000
$ 255,001 to 430,000	$ 119,000 + 60% of NW over $ 255,000
$ 430,001 or more	$ 224,000 + 100% of NW over $ 430,000

TABLE 5. ASSET PROTECTION ALLOWANCE
(Parents and Independent Students)

Age of older parent or student	Couple/ Married	Unmarried/ Single
25 or under	$ 0	$ 0
26	2,400	1,600
27	4,800	3,300
28	7,300	4,900
29	9,700	6,600
30	12,100	8,200
31	14,500	9,800
32	16,900	11,500
33	19,400	13,100
34	21,800	14,800
35	24,200	16,400
36	26,600	18,000
37	29,000	19,700
38	31,500	21,300
39	33,900	23,000
40	36,300	24,600
41	37,300	25,200
42	38,200	25,700
43	39,200	26,300
44	40,200	26,900
45	41,200	27,400
46	42,300	28,100
47	43,300	28,800
48	44,400	29,300
49	45,500	30,000
50	46,700	30,700
51	48,100	31,500
52	49,400	32,200
53	50,900	33,000
54	52,100	33,800
55	53,700	34,700
56	55,400	35,600
57	57,100	36,400
58	58,800	37,500
59	60,600	38,500
60	62,400	39,400
61	64,500	40,500
62	66,800	41,700
63	68,700	42,900
64	71,100	44,000
65 or over	73,500	45,500

TABLE 6. ASSET CONVERSION RATE
(Parents of Dependent Students/Independent Students with Dependents)

Asset conversion rate for Dependent Students and Independent Students with NO Dependents is 35%.

Asset conversion rate for Dependent Parents and Independent Students with Dependents is 12%.

TABLE 7. INCOME ASSESSMENT RATE
(Dependent Students/Independent Students with NO Dependents)

50% of available income

TABLE 8. CONTRIBUTION FROM ADJUSTED AVAILABLE INCOME (AAI)
(Parents of Dependent Students/Independent Students with Dependents)

Adjusted Available Income (AAI)	Total Contribution
Less than $-3,409	$ -750
$ -3,409 to 10,800	22% of AAI
$ 10,801 to 13,500	$2,376 + 25% of AAI over $ 10,800
$ 13,501 to 16,200	$3,051 + 29% of AAI over $ 13,500
$ 16,201 to 19,000	$3,834 + 34% of AAI over $ 16,200
$ 19,001 to 21,700	$4,786 + 40% of AAI over $ 19,000
$ 21,701 or more	$5,866 + 47% of AAI over $ 21,700

WORKSHEET 3: ESTIMATING FAMILY SHARE USING INSTITUTIONAL METHODOLOGY

Refer to the tables on pages 54 and 55 to complete this worksheet.

WORKSHEET 3: Parents

PARENTS' INCOME	
1. AGI/taxable income	$
2. Total untaxed income/benefits	+
3. Child support paid	−
4. Total parents' income (sum of lines 1 and 2, minus line 3)	=
ALLOWANCES	
5. U.S. income tax	
6. State and other taxes (% from Table 1 × line 4)	+
7. F.I.C.A. (Table 2)	+
8. Employment allowance (Table 2)	+
9. Medical/dental expense allowance (Table 2)	+
10. Income Protection Allowance (Table 3a)	+
11. Elementary/secondary tuition allowance (Table 2)	+
12. Total Allowances (sum of lines 5 to 11)	=
13. Available Income (line 4 minus line 12) may be negative	=
PARENTS' ASSETS	
14. Cash, savings, and checking accounts	
15. Investment equity	+
16. Home equity	+
17. Adjusted business/farm equity (Table 4)	+
18. Other real estate equity	+
19. Net Worth (sum of lines 14 to 18)	=
20. Asset Protection Allowance (Table 5)	−
21. Discretionary Net Worth (line 19 minus line 20)	=
22. Conversion percentage (Table 6 and line 21)	×
23. Income Supplement (line 21 × line 22); may be negative	=
24. Adjusted available income (sum of lines 13 and 23)	=
CONTRIBUTION	
25. TOTAL CONTRIBUTION (calculate using line 24 and Table 9); may be negative	=
26. Number of dependent children in college	÷
27. Parents' contribution for student (line 25 divided by line 26); cannot be negative	=

WORKSHEET 3 *continued*: Dependent Students

STUDENT'S INCOME	
1. Student's AGI/taxable income	$
2. Untaxed income/benefits	+
3. Taxable student aid	−
4. Total income (sum of lines 1 and 2, minus line 3)	=
ALLOWANCES	
5. U.S. income tax	
6. State and other taxes (% from Table 1 × line 1)	+
7. F.I.C.A. (Table 2)	+
8. Total Allowances (sum of lines 5, 6, and 7)	=
9. Available Income (line 4 minus line 8); cannot be less than $0	=
10. Contribution from income (line 9 × 50%, or Minimum Student Contribution from Table 8, whichever is greater)	=
STUDENT'S ASSETS	
11. Cash, savings, and checking accounts	
12. Investment equity	+
13. Home equity	+
14. Other real estate equity	+
15. Business/farm equity	+
16. Trust value	+
17. Net Worth (sum of lines 11 to 16)	+
18. Contribution from assets (line 17 × 35%; cannot be less than $0)	=
CONTRIBUTION	
19. TOTAL STUDENT'S CONTRIBUTION (sum of lines 10 and 18)	=

WORKSHEET 3 *continued*: Independent student with dependents (other than a spouse)

STUDENT'S (AND SPOUSE'S) INCOME	
1. AGI/taxable income	$
2. Total untaxed income/benefits	+
3. Income exclusions (Child support paid + taxable student aid)	−
4. Total income (sum of lines 1 and 2, minus line 3)	=
ALLOWANCES	
5. U.S. income tax	
6. State and other taxes (% from Table 1 × line 4)	+
7. F.I.C.A. (Table 2)	+
8. Employment allowance (Table 2)	+
9. Medical/dental allowance (Table 2)	+
10. Income Protection Allowance (Table 3a)	+
11. Total allowances (sum of lines 5 to 10)	=
12. Available Income (line 4 minus line 11; if less than $0, enter $0)	=
STUDENT'S (AND SPOUSE'S) ASSETS	
13. Cash, savings, and checking accounts	
14. Investment equity	+
15. Home equity	+
16. Other real estate equity	+
17. Adjusted business/farm equity (Table 4)	+
18. Trust value	+
19. Net Worth (sum of lines 13 to 18)	=
20. Asset Protection Allowance (Table 5)	−
21. Discretionary Net Worth (line 19 minus line 20)	=
22. Conversion percentage (Table 6 and line 21)	×
23. Income Supplement (line 21 × line 22); may be negative	=
24. Adjusted available income (sum of lines 12 and 23)	=
CONTRIBUTION	
25. TOTAL STUDENT'S CONTRIBUTION (calculate using line 24 and Table 9)	=
26. Number in college	÷
27. Contribution for student (line 25 divided by line 26, or Minimum Student Contribution from Table 8, whichever is greater)	=

WORKSHEET 3 *continued*: Independent student without dependents (other than a spouse)

STUDENT'S (AND SPOUSE'S) INCOME	
1. AGI/taxable income	$
2. Total untaxed income/benefits	+
3. Income exclusions (Child support paid + taxable student aid)	−
4. Total family income (sum of lines 1 and 2, minus line 3)	=
ALLOWANCES	
5. U.S. income tax	
6. State and other taxes (% from Table 1 times line 1)	+
7. F.I.C.A. (Table 2)	+
8. Employment allowance (Table 2)	+
9. Medical/dental expense allowance (Table 2)	+
10. Monthly Maintenance Allowance (Table 3b)	+
11. Total allowances (sum of lines 5 to 10)	=
12. Available income (line 4 minus line 11); may not be negative	=
13. Student's contribution from income (line 12 × 50% [divided by 2, if spouse enrolled] or $1,750, whichever is greater)	=
STUDENT'S (AND SPOUSE'S) ASSETS	
14. Cash, savings, and checking accounts	
15. Investment equity	+
16. Home equity	+
17. Other real estate equity	+
18. Adjusted business/farm equity (Table 4)	+
19. Trust value	+
20. Net Worth (sum of lines 14 to 19)	=
21. Asset Protection Allowance (Table 5)	−
22. Discretionary Net Worth (line 20 minus line 21)	=
23. Student's contribution from assets (line 22 × 35%, divided by 2 if spouse is enrolled; cannot be less than $0)	=
CONTRIBUTION	
24. TOTAL STUDENT'S CONTRIBUTION (sum of lines 13 and 23)	=

CHAPTER 4

1998-99 CSS
Institutional Methodology (IM)
Computation Tables

TABLE 1. ALLOWANCES FOR STATE AND OTHER TAXES

State/Territory/Country of Residence	Parents of Dependent Students and Independent Students with Dependents				Dependent and Independent w/ NO Dependents	
	Total Income				Taxable Income	
	$ 0- 20,000	$20,001- 40,000	$40,001- 60,000	$60,001- 80,000	$80,001 or more	$ 0- 20,000	$20,001 or more

State/Territory/Country of Residence	$0-20,000	$20,001-40,000	$40,001-60,000	$60,001-80,000	$80,001 or more	$0-20,000	$20,001 or more
Alabama (AL)	11 %	9 %	8 %	7 %	6 %	2 %	3 %
Alaska (AK)	5	4	3	3	3	0	0
American Samoa (AS)	4	3	3	3	3	0	0
Arizona (AZ)	14	10	9	8	8	1	2
Arkansas (AR)	12	9	9	9	8	2	2
California (CA)	14	9	9	9	10	0	1
Canada (CN)	9	8	8	8	8	4	5
Colorado (CO)	11	10	9	9	9	1	3
Connecticut (CT)	16	12	9	9	9	0	0
Delaware (DE)	7	7	7	7	8	2	3
District of Columbia (DC)	11	12	12	12	11	4	5
Federated States of Micronesia (FM)	4	3	3	3	3	0	0
Florida (FL)	13	8	7	5	5	0	0
Georgia (GA)	13	10	10	9	9	2	3
Guam (GU)	4	3	3	3	3	0	0
Hawaii (HI)	9	10	10	10	10	2	4
Idaho (ID)	12	10	10	10	10	1	2
Illinois (IL)	16	12	10	9	9	2	2
Indiana (IN)	15	10	9	9	8	3	3
Iowa (IA)	12	10	9	9	9	2	3
Kansas (KS)	13	10	9	8	8	1	2
Kentucky (KY)	12	10	10	9	9	4	4
Louisiana (LA)	13	10	8	8	7	1	1
Maine (ME)	12	10	10	10	10	0	1
Marshall Islands (MH)	4	3	3	3	3	0	0
Maryland (MD)	8	11	11	10	10	1	5
Massachusetts (MA)	14	12	11	11	11	3	4
Mexico (MX)	9	8	8	8	8	4	5
Michigan (MI)	14	12	11	11	11	3	4
Minnesota (MN)	10	11	10	10	10	1	3
Mississippi (MS)	11	9	8	8	7	1	1
Missouri (MO)	13	10	8	8	7	2	3
Montana (MT)	7	7	8	8	8	2	2
Nebraska (NE)	17	12	10	10	9	1	2
Nevada (NV)	10	6	5	4	4	0	0
New Hampshire (NH)	13	8	7	7	6	0	0
New Jersey (NJ)	15	12	11	11	11	1	2
New Mexico (NM)	12	10	9	9	9	1	1
New York (NY)	14	14	14	14	14	1	4
North Carolina (NC)	11	10	10	9	9	2	3
North Dakota (ND)	12	9	8	7	7	1	1
Northern Mariana Islands (MP)	4	3	3	3	3	0	0
Ohio (OH)	13	10	10	10	10	2	3
Oklahoma (OK)	12	10	9	9	8	2	3
Oregon (OR)	10	11	11	11	11	3	5
Palau (PW)	4	3	3	3	3	0	0
Pennsylvania (PA)	16	10	9	8	7	3	3
Puerto Rico (PR)	3	2	2	2	2	1	1
Rhode Island (RI)	14	12	11	11	11	1	2
South Carolina (SC)	10	9	9	9	8	1	2
South Dakota (SD)	14	9	7	6	5	0	0
Tennessee (TN)	14	8	6	6	5	0	0
Texas (TX)	15	9	7	6	6	0	0

TABLE 1., continued

State/Territory/Country of Residence	Parents of Dependent Students and Independent Students with Dependents				Dependent and Independent w/ NO Dependents	
	Total Income				Taxable Income	
	$ 0- 20,000	$20,001- 40,000	$40,001- 60,000	$60,001- 80,000	$80,001 or more	$ 0- 20,000	$20,001 or more

State/Territory/Country of Residence	$0-20,000	$20,001-40,000	$40,001-60,000	$60,001-80,000	$80,001 or more	$0-20,000	$20,001 or more
Utah (UT)	14	12	11	10	9	1	3
Vermont (VT)	7	9	9	9	9	0	2
Virgin Islands (VI)	4	3	3	3	3	0	0
Virginia (VA)	12	10	9	9	9	2	3
Washington (WA)	17	11	9	7	6	0	0
West Virginia (WV)	12	9	9	9	9	2	2
Wisconsin (WI)	12	14	13	12	11	1	4
Wyoming (WY)	9	6	5	4	4	0	0
Not Reported (NR)	13	10	9	9	8	1	2

TABLE 2. ALLOWANCES AGAINST INCOME

FICA: *Wages*

$1 to $65,400 .... 7.65% of income earned by each wage earner (maximum $5,003.10 per person)

$65,401 or more .... $5,003.10 + 1.45% of income earned above $65,400 by each wage earner

Elementary/secondary tuition allowance .... Reported tuition paid to maximum $5,990 per eligible child

Employment allowance .... 35% of lesser earned income to maximum $2,780 (single parent: 35% of earned income to maximum of $2,780)

Medical/dental expense allowance .... Unreimbursed expenses in excess of 4% of total income

TABLE 3a. INCOME PROTECTION ALLOWANCE (IPA)
(Parents of Dependent Students/Independent Students with Dependents)

Family Size* (including student)	Number in College**				
	1	2	3	4	5
2	$ 12,310	$ 10,390			
3	14,690	12,770	$ 10,850		
4	18,370	16,450	14,530	$ 12,610	
5	22,040	20,120	18,200	16,280	$ 14,360
6	25,530	23,610	21,690	19,770	17,850

* For each additional family member, add $3,310.
**For each additional college student, subtract $1,920.

TABLE 3b. MAINTENANCE ALLOWANCE
(Independent Students with NO Dependents)

Single Independent Student	$910 per month during period of nonenrollment
Married with NO Dependent Children	$570 per month during period of nonenrollment (calculated for student and spouse)

1998-99 CSS
Institutional Methodology (IM)
Computation Tables

TABLE 4. ADJUSTED NET WORTH OF A BUSINESS OR FARM

Net Worth (NW)		Adjusted Net Worth
Less than $1	$	0
$ 1 to 85,000	$	0 + 40% of NW
$ 85,001 to 255,000	$ 34,000	+ 50% of NW over $ 85,000
$ 255,001 to 430,000	$119,000	+ 60% of NW over $ 255,000
$ 430,001 or more	$224,000	+100% of NW over $ 430,000

TABLE 5. ASSET PROTECTION ALLOWANCE
(Parents and Independent Students)

Age of older parent or student	Couple/ Married	Unmarried/ Single
25 or under	$ 0	$ 0
26	2,300	1,400
27	4,500	2,800
28	6,800	4,100
29	9,100	5,500
30	11,300	6,900
31	13,600	8,200
32	15,900	9,600
33	18,100	11,000
34	20,400	12,400
35	22,700	13,700
36	24,900	15,100
37	27,200	16,500
38	29,500	17,900
39	31,700	19,200
40	34,000	20,600
41	35,200	21,400
42	36,500	22,100
43	37,800	22,900
44	39,100	23,700
45	40,500	24,600
46	41,900	25,400
47	43,400	26,300
48	45,000	27,300
49	46,600	28,200
50	48,200	29,200
51	50,200	30,400
52	52,000	31,500
53	54,100	32,800
54	56,300	34,200
55	58,300	35,400
56	60,700	36,800
57	63,200	38,300
58	65,700	39,800
59	68,700	41,700
60	71,500	43,300
61	74,700	45,300
62	77,700	47,100
63	81,100	49,200
64	84,700	51,400
65	88,400	53,600
66 or over	92,300	56,000

TABLE 6. ASSET CONVERSION RATE
(Parents of Dependent Students/Independent Students with Dependents)

IF discretionary net worth is	AND available income (AI) is	THEN conversion percentage is
$0 or more	Any amount	12%
Less than $0	$29,200 or more	0%
Less than $0	$1–29,199	$6\% \times \dfrac{29,200-AI}{29,200}$
Less than $0	$0 or less	6%

Asset conversion rate for Dependent Students and Independent Students with NO Dependents is 35%.

TABLE 7. INCOME ASSESSMENT RATE
(Dependent Students/Independent Students with NO Dependents)

50% of available income

TABLE 8. STUDENT'S MINIMUM STANDARD CONTRIBUTION

$ 1,050 .... Freshman: Dependent/Independent with Dependents

1,300 .... All Other Students: Dependent/Independent with Dependents

1,750 .... Independent Students with NO Dependents

TABLE 9. CONTRIBUTION FROM ADJUSTED AVAILABLE INCOME (AAI)
(Parents of Dependent Students/Independent Students with Dependents)

Adjusted Available Income (AAI)	Total Contribution
Less than $ -3,409	$ -750
$ -3,409 to 10,800	22% of AAI
$ 10,801 to 13,500	$ 2,376 + 25% of AAI over $ 10,800
$ 13,501 to 16,200	$ 3,051 + 29% of AAI over $ 13,500
$ 16,201 to 19,000	$ 3,834 + 34% of AAI over $ 16,200
$ 19,001 to 21,700	$ 4,786 + 40% of AAI over $ 19,000
$ 21,701 or more	$ 5,866 + 47% of AAI over $ 21,700

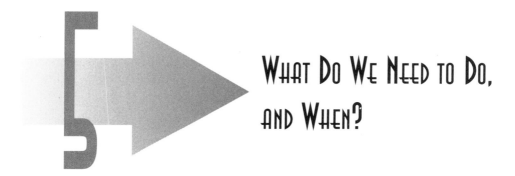

What Do We Need to Do, and When?

Now that you have an idea of the college costs your family faces, the kinds of financing options available, and how your family's financial situation will be viewed by the others in the partnership, you'll want to know how to make sure you apply for funding in a timely way.

Don't forget to meet the deadlines for admission application materials, too. The most accurate and timely financial aid applications will be of no use if your child does not meet admission deadlines!

Unless you look forward to filling out your income tax forms every year, you probably won't find filling out financial aid forms much fun either. But the potential payoff for your child should help see you through the process. And you'll only have to fill out the FAFSA, and CSS/Financial Aid PROFILE if it is used by your child's college choices, once each year. Information on the FAFSA and PROFILE will be sent to all the colleges your child lists on the forms as possible college choices.

A note about Early Decision and Early Action admission programs: If your child is applying to his or her first-choice college under one of these early plans, it is especially important to find out from the college what the deadlines for aid consideration are. Often you have to complete aid forms before you have the benefit of official income tax information; you simply estimate as accurately as you can what your financial situation will be by the end of the tax year. The college will use this estimated information to determine any financial aid package, which will be altered, if necessary, after your year-end information has been reported on the FAFSA or other required forms.

The early bird gets the worm.

Actually, it's not so much that the early bird gets the worm as the late bird gets little or nothing. While it is critical to adhere to the priority deadlines established by each college for its financial aid application process, sending in hurriedly completed information—or a FAFSA before January 1—may well delay you in the process while inaccuracies are corrected or numbers adjusted. Perhaps you should revise this thinking to "the timely bird gets the worm."

A GENERAL CALENDAR FOR COMPLETING THE FINANCIAL AID APPLICATION PROCESS

While the very best source of information about the forms you'll need to file—and when you will need to file them—will be the financial aid offices at the colleges to which your child is applying, it is important to understand the general sequence of the financial aid application process. It is outlined below.

1. No later than fall of the senior year of high school, your child should gather admission and financial aid information from colleges of interest. Determine which financial aid application forms your family will be required to file to qualify for aid, and get copies of the forms.

    The FAFSA will be available in the late fall in your high school guidance office or from the financial aid office at colleges.

➤ The PROFILE Registration Guide will also be available in your child's high school guidance office or from colleges using the service.

➤ College financial aid forms, when required, will be available directly from the college and are often included in the admission application materials.

2. If applying to one or more colleges that use PROFILE, register for your customized Application. The PROFILE Registration Guide includes a worksheet to fill out so that you'll have the necessary information when you register. Registration is done by phone, through College Board Online™, or through ExPAN, the College Board's electronic guidance and application network. Registrations are accepted beginning September 15 of the year prior to your child's intended college enrollment.

3. Within 7 to 10 days of registering for your customized PROFILE Application, your child will receive a personalized packet of PROFILE forms and instructions.

4. Complete the PROFILE, if required, and return the form in time for CSS® to receive it by your earliest college-specified financial aid deadline. (See the customized letter that accompanies the PROFILE Application.)

5. Mail the completed FAFSA after January 1 of the college enrollment year, but at least four weeks before the earliest financial aid deadline set by the college or state scholarship or grant programs to which your child is applying.

6. Complete and return any other required financial aid application forms.

7. Within four weeks of submitting the FAFSA, your child will receive from the U.S. Department of Education his or her Student Aid Report (SAR), which includes the federal government's determination of your expected family contribution and lists the information you reported on the FAFSA. If you find any errors, be sure to correct them and return the form right away so that the corrected information can be sent to the colleges where your child is applying.

8. Once the PROFILE Application has been processed, your child will receive a CSS Acknowledgment containing the following information:

➤ The Acknowledgment confirms the colleges and programs that will be receiving the PROFILE information.

➤ The Additional School Request section of the Acknowledgment enables applicants to report PROFILE information to other colleges and programs that were not included during registration.

➤ The Data Confirmation section of the Acknowledgment provides a record of the information the family submitted for PROFILE processing and reporting. Changes or corrections to the information in the Data Confirmation section can be submitted directly to college financial aid offices.

When you fill out financial aid application forms, you will want to be as complete and accurate as you can about indicating your financial circumstances. If you omit requested information, or use different figures for such items as income or savings on different aid application forms, the extra time needed to supply the correct information will delay your child's application.

It's so complicated, we'll have to hire a financial adviser.

While the financial aid application process can be time-consuming, it generally becomes complicated only if you and your child don't allow enough time to find out what's required and then do it. If you read this book as well as information from your child's college choices carefully, you should have in hand what you need to complete the process successfully. The instructions that accompany both the FAFSA and the CSS/Financial Aid PROFILE are detailed and comprehensive.

For more information on the application process:

Admission and financial aid offices at colleges of interest

College and university Web sites

High school guidance counselors

Questions Families Should Ask About What They Need to Do, and When

Financial aid administrators at the colleges your child is considering will be able to give you the answers to these questions. The worksheet on page 62 will help you keep track of the dates required materials are due—and keep you on track during the financial aid application process.

1. What financial aid forms are required by this college?

2. When are the forms due to be completed and returned to the processor and/or college?

3. Will a copy of parents' and/or students' tax forms be required? If so, by when?

4. When will we receive notification of the college's financial aid decision?

5. What is the deadline for accepting the financial aid award?

WORKSHEET 4: TRACKING YOUR FINANCIAL AID APPLICATION REQUIREMENTS

	Required Forms	Due Date/ Deadline	Date Completed
Institution			
FAFSA	_____	_____	_____
PROFILE			
• Registration	_____	_____	_____
• Application	_____	_____	_____
College Forms	_____	_____	_____
Tax Forms	_____	_____	_____
Other	_____	_____	_____
Institution			
FAFSA	_____	_____	_____
PROFILE			
• Registration	_____	_____	_____
• Application	_____	_____	_____
College Forms	_____	_____	_____
Tax Forms	_____	_____	_____
Other	_____	_____	_____
Institution			
FAFSA	_____	_____	_____
PROFILE			
• Registration	_____	_____	_____
• Application	_____	_____	_____
College Forms	_____	_____	_____
Tax Forms	_____	_____	_____
Other	_____	_____	_____
Institution			
FAFSA	_____	_____	_____
PROFILE			
• Registration	_____	_____	_____
• Application	_____	_____	_____
College Forms	_____	_____	_____
Tax Forms	_____	_____	_____
Other	_____	_____	_____

Be sure to submit required admission applications on time as well. Financial aid decisions are not made until a student is accepted for admission.

WHAT DOES THIS AID PACKAGE REALLY MEAN?

If you and your child have followed the admission and financial aid application time lines for the colleges to which he or she decided to apply—and your child was realistic about the likelihood of admission—chances are there will be more than one "fat envelope" arriving in your mailbox in the spring of senior year. If your circumstances warrant it, these acceptance materials will include a financial aid award.

Many families are surprised each year to find differences—sometimes quite significant ones—between the financial aid awards offered by different colleges. These families think they know what their "need" will be, and expect that financial aid from each school will include a similar plan for covering the difference between the cost of attendance and the expected family contribution.

But, having read this far, you realize that Institutional Methodology is not a strict formula that all colleges use to determine need (as compared with the Federal Methodology, which determines eligibility for federal funds). And there is no specific formula governing how all the colleges will "package" the financial aid that students and families are offered. There is, however, likely to be a formula that each *individual* college has developed to award its limited financial aid resources.

When you find differences in calculated need and in the terms of financial aid awarded, you can be sure the professional judgment of the college's financial aid administrator came into play. Based on their experience with other families in similar circumstances, financial aid administrators may use their own judgment to interpret a family's financial data differently than the standard methodology might suggest.

A financial aid package is the total financial aid award received by a student; it may be made up of a combination of aid that includes both gift aid and self-help. Because it is likely that the financial aid packages your child receives will be at least slightly different, it will be important for you get them all in hand and review them with some key criteria in mind. You'll want to compare apples to apples insofar as you are able. For example, a total aid package of $20,000 may seem on the face of it to be preferable to one totaling $15,000. But you'll need to compare the actual components of the packages to determine which is better for you and your child in the long run.

FACTORS TO CONSIDER IN COMPARING OFFERS
Percentage of Grant Aid versus Loan

In general, the higher the proportion of grant aid versus loan aid, the more attractive the package will be in the long term. Students will have fewer debts to repay and the cost of attending college will be lower. More attractive packages are often offered to students in whom colleges are most interested. In fact, some colleges will offer a package of near-total grant aid for the students they most want to come to their campus.

Percentage of Self-Help versus Grant Aid

This is a broader way of comparing aid packages than by looking strictly at grant versus loan. Self-help includes not only the expected family contribution and the loans that are offered in the aid package but also any student employment monies that are included. While there may well be advantages to working on campus beyond financial ones, some families feel that an aid package that does not include the expectation that the student work during the academic year is preferable to one that does. You'll also want to compare the colleges' expectations for summer earnings and be realistic about whether your child will be able to earn what each college is expecting.

Terms of Loans

Student loans based on financial need, with low interest rates and no expected payments until after the student graduates or leaves college, are preferable to unsubsidized loans or loans your child might be recommended to take out from private lending sources.

Gapping

This term refers to the process by which a "gap" is left unfilled in the aid package between the cost of attendance and the family's expected contribution. If your child has been "gapped" at a particular college, it means that your family would be expected to find this money somewhere else if your child were to enroll. It is important to compare the proportion of unmet need (or gap), if any, in evaluating financial aid award packages.

While you are involved in interpreting and comparing your child's financial aid awards, be sure to keep in mind the deadlines set by the colleges for acceptance of awards. If you miss the deadline, your child's financial aid package could be offered to another student. You should also bear in mind that your child is not required to accept the entire aid package as offered. But if he or she does decline a part of it, such as the work-study opportunity, the college may not be able to restore that aid if your child changes his or her mind later.

You don't need to let yourself be pressured into making an immediate decision about whether to accept an aid offer. If necessary, contact the financial aid office and request an extension of the deadline. (For information on what to do if you believe the financial aid package offered will not provide enough assistance, see Chapter 7.)

CHAPTER 6

The case studies that follow will give you an idea of the amount of variation you might find in your child's financial aid packages and provide clues for interpreting various awards. The worksheet at the end of this chapter provides a tool for comparing apples to apples once your child receives his or her financial aid offers.

COMPARING FINANCIAL AID PACKAGES

 SARAH SMITH

	Prairie	Old Bricks	Central
Cost of Attendance	$ 7,835	$19,035	$16,260
Family Contribution	2,352	2,352	2,352
Contribution from non-custodial parent	—	1,500	—
Financial Need	$ 5,483	$15,183	$13,908
Financial Aid Packages			
Federal Pell Grant	$ 400	$ 400	$ 400
State Scholarship Grant	200	1,000	800
Institutional Grant	400	7,150	7,583
Private Scholarship	1,000	1,000	1,000
Federal Perkins Loan	2,000	1,000	0
Federal Stafford or Direct Loan	0	2,625	2,625
Federal Work-Study	1,200	2,000	1,500
TOTAL AWARD	**$5,200**	**$15,175**	**$13,908**

When comparing the financial aid packages Sarah received, she and her mother noted three key points to consider:

➤ *Noncustodial parent contribution*: Old Bricks was the only college to request financial information from Sarah's father, and the financial aid office there is expecting him to contribute $1,500 toward Sarah's freshman-year cost of attendance. The other colleges do not have this same expectation. This is one of the areas where colleges have the option to customize their aid policies to make institutional funds go farther. In making a final decision about where to attend, this is a factor Sarah and her mother will need to consider.

➤ *Whether need is met*: Old Bricks and Central have offered Sarah aid packages that virtually meet her demonstrated need. Prairie has offered a package that leaves $283 of her need unmet; there is a "gap" between the aid award and her financial need. Some institutions meet full need and others do not; it is an institutional decision, based in large part on the financial aid budget at the college. Sarah and her mother will need to take this into consideration, and find another source of funding to cover the gap should Sarah decide to enroll at Prairie.

➤ *Loan expectations*: Both Prairie and Central expect that Sarah will borrow from one loan program; Old Bricks includes two loans in the package. Higher-cost institutions often require that students borrow more. This is another factor for Sarah and her mother to consider, in light of what her earning potential may be after college and how much of a debt burden she can realistically carry.

JAMES WASHINGTON

	Colony	Very Old Bricks	Division
Cost of Attendance	$10,980	$25,720	$17,325
Family Contribution	(FM) 11,351	(IM) 10,097	(FM) 11,351
Financial Need	$ 0	$15,623	$ 5,974
Financial Aid Packages			
Federal Pell Grant	$ 0	$ 0	$ 0
State Scholarship Grant	0	500	400
Institutional Grant	0	8,500	1,449
Private Scholarship	0	0	0
Federal Perkins Loan	0	2,000	0
Federal Stafford or			
Direct Loan	0	2,625	2,625
Federal Work-Study	0	1,500	1,500
TOTAL AWARD	$ 0	$15,125	$ 5,974

These are the key points James and his family are considering in comparing the financial aid offers he received:

➤ *Family contribution*: Colony and Division used Federal Methodology in determining James's financial need, whereas Very Old Bricks used Institutional Methodology. The family contribution expected from Very Old Bricks takes into consideration the substantial unreimbursed medical expenses incurred by James's family and illustrates how Institutional Methodology can be more sensitive to individual family circumstances. James and his family may want to appeal the aid decisions at Colony and Division, documenting the high medical expenses that were not taken into account in the analysis.

➤ *Grants versus the big picture*: At first glance, the $8,500 grant from Very Old Bricks looks dramatically better than the $1,449 grant offered by

Division. But Division has met James's family's demonstrated need, whereas Very Old Bricks has a higher loan expectation and has also left a $500 gap between the aid offer and the expected family contribution. James and his family will need to consider which offer is really better for the family; it may not necessarily be the one containing the bigger grant.

➤ *Cost of attendance*: Even though Colony has offered James no financial aid, it may turn out to be the most realistic choice from a purely financial point of view. The cost of attendance for Colony is less than the expected family contribution at Division; and the loan and work requirements built into the Very Old Bricks package make it more costly in the long run. James's family might be able to finance the family contribution at Colony in such a way that it makes little impact on their current income and lifestyle.

MARIA
MARTINEZ

	Canyon	Major Mortar	Midway
Cost of Attendance	$ 5,525	$21,730	$18,050
Family Contribution	(FM) 16,335	(IM) 18,153	(IM) 18,153
Financial Need	$ 0	$ 3,577	$ 0
Financial Aid Packages			
Federal Pell Grant	$ 0	$ 0	$ 0
State Scholarship Grant	0	0	0
Institutional Grant	0	1,077	0
Private Scholarship	2,500	2,500	2,500
Federal Perkins Loan	0	0	0
Federal Stafford or Direct Loan	0	0	0
Federal Work-Study	0	0	0
TOTAL AWARD	$ 2,500	$ 3,577	$ 2,500

Other financing alternatives not based on financial need or student merit suggested by Maria's college choices:

	Canyon	Major Mortar	Midway
Federal PLUS Loan (Up to cost of attendance minus financial aid)	yes	yes	yes
Institutional Payment Plan	no	yes	yes
Institutional Loan (to replace family contribution)	no	yes	no
Home Equity Line of Credit	yes	yes	yes

Given what Maria and her parents had estimated their expected family contribution would be, they are not surprised by the little financial aid they have been offered by the colleges to which she was admitted. However, there are some key factors for consideration as Maria makes her college choice:

➡ *Cost of attendance/private scholarship*: The outside scholarship Maria received from an organization supporting Hispanic women majoring in the sciences makes a more dramatic difference at Canyon, her least expensive option (where it cuts her costs almost in half) than it does at the other two colleges. If she continues to receive the scholarship throughout her college years, Canyon would cost less for four years than Major Mortar or Midway would cost for one year. (Maria might also want to find out if the—currently need-based—athletic scholarship she has been offered from Major Mortar would increase in future years if she excels on the college tennis team.)

➡ *Financing alternatives*: Maria's parents will want to look into a variety of options for financing college costs. The institutional payment plans offered at Major Mortar and Midway would help them spread the costs over the calendar year, rather than the two lump-sum semester payments required at Canyon. Major Mortar also sponsors an institutional loan program that might offer generous terms. If Maria is seriously considering

Major Mortar or Midway, it's likely her parents will investigate a Federal PLUS Loan or establish a line of credit based on their home equity.

If it can sometimes be difficult to justify the differences in the financial aid packages your child receives, it is even more problematic to try to compare the aid your child receives with what the student down the street received. It's not uncommon for parents to complain that "John Doe, whose parents are in the same income bracket, received more aid than my child." By now you realize that a lot of other factors may well have been involved. You'll do best to save your energy and devote it to ensuring that your child makes the most of the financial aid opportunities afforded him or her.

For more information on comparing award offers:

Admission and financial aid offices at the colleges where your child was admitted

College Costs and Financial Aid Handbook, 1998

College Board Online: *www.collegeboard.org*

High school guidance counselor

Questions Families Should Ask Colleges About the Aid Package

Many colleges provide a helpful enclosure with financial aid awards, explaining the college's financial aid packaging philosophy and the factors that went into determining the family's expected contribution and financial need. Such enclosures often include detailed information about facets of the aid package such as loan terms and sources. If you don't find such information accompanying a college's financial aid award, you may want to ask the financial aid office some of the following questions.

1. What are the terms (interest, repayment policies) of the loans that are part of this aid package?

2. How likely are we to qualify for the parent loans that are part of this package?

3. What if my child decides he or she would like to work more hours than are included in this aid package?

4. If my child declines the work portion of this aid package, what are the chances of getting a work-study job later if my child changes his or her mind?

5. What are recommended sources of additional funding to cover the gap (if any) between what our family can afford and what the aid package covers?

6. Is it possible to get an extension of the financial aid acceptance deadline to more thoroughly compare the aid awards my child has received?

7. How will any outside scholarships my child might be awarded after accepting this offer affect the aid package?

8. If our family financial situation and this college's costs remain essentially the same, how will grant and loan amounts change during the years my child is enrolled?

WORKSHEET 5: COMPARING AWARD LETTERS

STEP 1

List the name of each school you would like to attend, the award deadline date, and the total cost of attendance. This information should be in your award letter. If not, refer to the college catalog to estimate the cost of attendance, or call the financial aid office.

	College 1	College 2	College 3	College 4
Name of College	_____	_____	_____	_____
Award Deadline Date	_____	_____	_____	_____
Total Cost of Attendance	$_____	$_____	$_____	$_____

STEP 2

List the financial aid awards each school is offering. Do not forget that grants, scholarships, and work-study *do not* have to be repaid, while all loans *must* be repaid.

Grants and Scholarships

	College 1	College 2	College 3	College 4
Federal Pell	$_____	$_____	$_____	$_____
Federal SEOG	$_____	$_____	$_____	$_____
State	$_____	$_____	$_____	$_____
College	$_____	$_____	$_____	$_____
Other	$_____	$_____	$_____	$_____
TOTAL Grants and Scholarships	_____	_____	_____	_____
Percent of package that is grant	_____%	_____%	_____%	_____%

Work-Study Opportunities

	College 1	College 2	College 3	College 4
Work-Study Opportunities	$_____	$_____	$_____	$_____

Loans

	College 1	College 2	College 3	College 4
Federal Stafford	$_____	$_____	$_____	$_____
Federal Perkins	$_____	$_____	$_____	$_____
Other	$_____	$_____	$_____	$_____
TOTAL Loans	$_____	$_____	$_____	$_____
Percent of package that is self-help	_____%	_____%	_____%	_____%

WORKSHEET 5 *continued*

Total Financial Aid Award
Grants and Scholarships+
Work-Study + Loans= $_____ $_____ $_____ $_____

STEP 3

Calculate what it will cost you to attend the college you are considering. For each college, enter the total cost of attendance. Then, subtract the total financial aid award from the total cost of attendance. That number is the net cost, or what it will cost you to attend that school.

A. Total Cost
   of Attendance $_____ $_____ $_____ $_____

B. Total Financial Aid
   Award $_____ $_____ $_____ $_____

C. Net Cost to Attend $_____ $_____ $_____ $_____
   (A minus B = C)

WHAT DO WE DO IF THE AID PACKAGE IS NOT ENOUGH?

After careful review of the financial aid packages your child receives, you may be convinced that the contribution expected of your family is not at all realistic. You may decide that further follow-up is warranted with your child's first-choice college to see if other arrangements might be made to help you meet college costs. Before doing this, however, you should be aware that the majority of colleges have limited funds and a strict campus policy for awarding them, as well as a written policy about adjustments that can be made to the family contribution.

APPEAL STRATEGIES

If you decide to appeal the financial aid award your child has received, you will first need to contact the college financial aid office to find out what process, if any, they employ in reviewing financial aid awards. At this point, you should be prepared to discuss any special circumstances that may have been overlooked. Most financial aid administrators will request that special circumstances or changes in income or other data that have occurred since the time of your application for aid be put in writing, even if they are willing to discuss the situation by phone first. Whatever the case, be sure to follow the college's guidelines for appealing an award, so that you will not delay the process.

Be sure that you have data to back up your concerns about how much the college is expecting you to pay, not just emotion. Few aid officers are impressed by unsubstantiated whining!

If you are able to provide substantive new information, or a valuable reinterpretation of old data, it is possible that the financial aid administrator may be able to adjust your child's award to make meeting college costs more feasible. You'll need to bear in mind that financial aid officers must constantly prioritize the needs of the many families who ask for assistance. Even if you have a demonstrated need for additional aid, there may be other families with greater needs who must be served.

Most colleges will bargain with families about the aid decision.

While many colleges will listen to an informed and data-based appeal, it is not true that most colleges will bargain. Although there are a few exceptions, most financial aid officers are governed by strict campus policies that attempt to ensure equitable awards for all deserving applicants. They can, of course, use their professional judgment to make warranted adjustments in a package that was put together without knowledge of special circumstances. But you should not approach the comparison of your award packages as the basis for "let's make a deal" negotiations.

OTHER FINANCING OPTIONS

There are two categories of families who are likely to find alternative funding sources attractive:

- those who demonstrate no financial need but are looking for ways to reduce the impact of college costs on their day-to-day lifestyle

- those who are not completely satisfied with the amount of aid available to them through the college's financial aid package

In either case, there are a variety of options to consider. Details about these programs can be found in Chapter 3.

Unsubsidized Federal Loans

These loans are awarded through participating colleges (Federal Direct Loans) or from a bank (Federal Family Educational Loans/Stafford).

Federal PLUS Loans

You can borrow any amount between the cost of attendance and any aid your child has already received.

Privately Funded Student and Parent Loans

There are a variety of commercial sources for loans that are not based on need but on ability to repay (see table on page 79).

Student Employment

Even if your child does not qualify for a need-based job, he or she may be able to get a job on campus or a part-time job off campus. For most students, the days of being able to work one's way through college are over, but part-time work can help meet some of the costs for personal expenses or books.

When your child looks for a part-time job, it is important to keep in mind that campus employers are likely to be more flexible than off-campus employers about work hours during exam weeks and vacation periods.

Tuition Payment Plans

These plans fall into two general categories:

- those that allow parents to spread payment of college costs throughout the year

- prepayment plans, for those who can afford the total four-year cost in advance to avoid any future inflation-related increases

Some tuition payment plans are college-based, while others are commercial plans that may be recommended by the college.

Some colleges permit families to use a credit card for tuition payments. This permits families to accumulate benefits (such as airline or hotel points) through their affinity credit cards, which may make payment a little less painful. Consider using those airline points to pay for your child's trip home at the end of the year!

LEADING PRIVATE LOANS AT A GLANCE

Name and Sponsor	Maximum Amount	Credit Requirements	Rate	Maximum Term	Fees	Principal Deferral
ExtraCredit* The College Board 800-874-9390	Cost of education minus financial aid.	Good credit history and ability to repay.	8.5% until May 1997; then 91-day T-bill rate plus 4.5%, adjusted quarterly. Recent rate: 9.1%	15 years	3%	No
ExtraTime™ The College Board 800-874-9390	Cost of education minus financial aid.	Good credit history and ability to repay.	91-day T-bill rate plus 4.5%, adjusted quarterly. Recent rate: 9.75%	10 years	opt. 1=4% opt. 2=3%	Yes

AchieverLoan
Knight College
Resource Group
800-225-6783
  a) Multiple Year Option
  b) Annual Option
  c) Interest Only Option
	Cost of education minus financial aid.	Good credit history and ability to repay.	91-day T-bill rate plus 4.5%, adjusted quarterly. Multiple Year Option: 9.16% for first year. Recent rate: 9.75%	15 years	a) 3%
					b) 3%
					c) 4%
						a) No
						b) No
						c) Yes

TERI The Education Resources Institute 800-255-8374	$2,000 up to cost of education minus financial aid.	Good credit history and ability to repay; parents may act as cosigner.	Prime rate plus 0%, adjusted monthly. Recent rate: 8.25%	25 years	No fee	Yes
PLATO University Support Services 800-467-5286 800-GO-PLATO	$25,000 a year.	Annual income of $15,000, good credit history, and ability to repay. Parents can cosign for students.	Prime rate plus 1.9%, adjusted monthly. Recent rate: 10.15% Ask about our 7.9% introductory rate!	15 years	7%	Yes
EXCEL Nellie Mae 800-634-9308	Cost of education minus financial aid.	Good credit history and ability to repay. Parents can cosign for students.	Monthly variable rate year 1: prime + .5%. Current rate = 8.75%. After first year: prime + 1%. Current rate = 9.25%. Annual renewal rate = 10.75%	20 years	7%	Yes
EducaidEXTRA **Premier Loan** Educaid 916-554-8517	Cost of education minus financial aid up to $60,000[1].	Good credit history and ability to repay. Student/cosigner must have annual income of $15,000.	52 week T-bill + 3.10% reset quarterly, rounded to nearest 1/8th.	15 years[2]	5%[3] 6%[4]	Yes

[1] can be taken in one year.

[2] can defer repayment of interest up to five years after initial disbursement of first loan.

[3] if you start immediate repayment.

[4] if repayment is deferred.

CALCULATING YOUR MONTHLY LOAN PAYMENT

This chart illustrates repayment over 10 years for various loan amounts and interest rates. To calculate a monthly payment for a loan amount other than those on the chart, multiply the amount borrowed times the repayment factor for your interest rate. For example, if you borrowed $12,500 at 7.5%, your monthly payment would be $148.46 ($12,500 x .0118770).

Amount of Loan	Interest Rate		Repayment Factor		Monthly Payment
$10,000	7.00%	x	.011611	=	$116.11
	7.25%	x	.011740	=	$117.40
	7.50%	x	.011870	=	$118.70
	7.75%	x	.012001	=	$120.01
	8.00%	x	.012133	=	$121.33
	8.25%	x	.012265	=	$122.65
	8.50%	x	.012399	=	$123.99
	8.75%	x	.012533	=	$125.33
	9.00%	x	.012668	=	$126.68
$20,000	7.00%	x	.011611	=	$232.22
	7.25%	x	.011740	=	$234.80
	7.50%	x	.011870	=	$237.40
	7.75%	x	.012001	=	$240.02
	8.00%	x	.012133	=	$242.66
	8.25%	x	.012265	=	$245.30
	8.50%	x	.012399	=	$247.98
	8.75%	x	.012533	=	$250.66
	9.00%	x	.012668	=	$253.36
$30,000	7.00%	x	.011611	=	$348.33
	7.25%	x	.011740	=	$352.22
	7.50%	x	.011870	=	$356.10
	7.75%	x	.012001	=	$360.03
	8.00%	x	.012133	=	$363.99
	8.25%	x	.012265	=	$367.95
	8.50%	x	.012399	=	$371.97
	8.75%	x	.012533	=	$375.99
	9.00%	x	.012668	=	$380.04

For more information on other financing resources:

College Board Online: *www.collegeboard.org*

College Costs and Financial Aid Handbook, 1998

Financial aid and business offices at colleges of interest

Questions Families Should Ask Colleges When the Aid Package Is Not Enough

If there is a significant discrepancy between what you believe your family can afford and what the college has offered as a financial aid package, you may want to contact the college financial aid office to ask the following questions:

1. Is it possible to appeal this financial aid package?

2. What are the criteria for making an appeal?

3. What procedures should we follow in making an appeal?

4. What alternative funding sources would you recommend?

5. What financing plans are available?

CHAPTER 7

WORKSHEET 6: DEBT PLANNING FOR BORROWERS FROM FEDERAL PLUS AND PRIVATE SUPPLEMENTAL LOAN PROGRAMS

Some parents elect to borrow from private loan programs, sometimes called "supplemental" or "alternative" loan programs. Most of these programs make loans on the basis of the applicant's credit history and debt-to-income ratio. The criteria for determining whether an applicant is creditworthy are always more stringent in private loan programs than in the Federal PLUS program.

This worksheet, prepared by the College Board's CollegeCredit™ Education Loan Program, explains the credit history review process and will help you determine your debt-to-income ratio.

Your Credit History

In preparing to pay for college, you should maintain a good credit history that complies with industry standards. Check your credit history periodically to ensure that your records are accurate and up-to-date. Errors and inconsistencies can occur, particularly when a person's name or address changes. Resolve any problems as soon as you identify them. You may wish to check with your lender before you submit an application to determine whether there are any particular criteria (beyond the industry standards) that you will need to meet.

Your Debt-to-Income Ratio

Calculating your debt-to-income ratio is one way that a lender determines how much *additional* debt you can handle, based on your current income and obligations. The following worksheet explains how to compute your own debt-to-income ratio. The industry standard, as reflected in the following worksheet, is 37 percent. However, some lenders maintain higher or lower ratios.

WORKSHEET 6 *continued*

To compute your *current* debt-to-income ratio:

Step 1

    Current monthly gross income   _____

  x .037 industry standard for manageable debt

  = Portion of monthly gross income available
     for debt payments   =   _____

Step 2

    Monthly rent or mortgage payment   _____

  + Monthly car payment   _____

  + Minimum monthly payment on installment loan(s)   _____

  + Minimum monthly payment on all credit cards   _____

  = Total monthly payments   =   _____

Step 3

    37% of monthly gross income
    (result from Step 1)   _____

  — Total monthly payments (result from Step 2)   _____

  = Available for additional monthly debt payment =   _____

Ask your lender how much your minimum monthly payment will be for the supplemental loan you are considering. If that amount is larger than the amount remaining at the end of Step 3, you *and* your lender may have reason to be concerned about your ability to manage the added debt.

WORKSHEET 7: CASH-FLOW WORKSHEET FOR PARENT BORROWERS

Many parents find they must borrow to help send their children to college. But before you take out a Federal PLUS Loan, it's important to understand your cash flow and know exactly how much you can afford to repay each month.

This worksheet was prepared by the College Board's CollegeCredit Education Loan Program to help parents calculate their monthly expenses and estimate their monthly cash on hand.

MONTHLY FAMILY EXPENSES

Housing and Maintenance
- ❏ Mortgage or rent payment $ _____
- ❏ Electricity _____
- ❏ Gas _____
- ❏ Water and sewer _____
- ❏ Telephone _____
- ❏ Property taxes _____
- ❏ Homeowner's insurance _____
- ❏ Household help _____
- ❏ Furniture and appliances _____
- ❏ Other household items _____
- ❏ Home maintenance _____
- ❏ Other _____

Family
- ❏ Groceries $ _____
- ❏ School lunches _____
- ❏ Clothing _____
- ❏ Laundry and dry cleaning _____
- ❏ Toiletries _____
- ❏ Prescription drugs _____
- ❏ Child care _____
- ❏ Education expenses _____
- ❏ Children's camp expenses _____
- ❏ Children's allowance _____
- ❏ Gifts _____
- ❏ Medical expenses _____
- ❏ Medical insurance _____
- ❏ Dental expenses _____

Subtotal Monthly Expenses $ _____

Subtotal from previous column $ _____
- ❏ Dental insurance _____
- ❏ Life insurance _____
- ❏ Other _____

Transportation
- ❏ Automobile payments $ _____
- ❏ Gasoline _____
- ❏ Auto insurance _____
- ❏ Auto maintenance _____
- ❏ Other _____

Leisure
- ❏ Movies and theater $ _____
- ❏ Cable television _____
- ❏ Books/magazines/newspapers _____
- ❏ Vacations _____
- ❏ Restaurants _____
- ❏ Club memberships _____
- ❏ Other _____

Other
- ❏ Installment loans $ _____
- ❏ Credit card debt not accounted for above _____
- ❏ Investment expenses _____
- ❏ Accountant's fees _____
- ❏ Attorney's fees _____
- ❏ Charitable and political contributions _____
- ❏ Other _____

TOTAL Monthly Expenses $ _____

WORKSHEET 7 *continued*

Monthly Income
❏ Net monthly income after
taxes and payroll deductions $ _____
❏ Rent paid to you   _____
❏ Alimony received   _____
❏ Interest and divided income   _____

TOTAL Monthly Income $ _____

TOTAL Monthly Income	$ _____
Minus	
TOTAL Monthly Expenses	$ _____
Equals	
Cash on Hand After	
Monthly Expenses	$ _____

NOTE: Financial planners suggest that a family's outstanding debt should not be greater than 38 to 40 percent of the family's net income.

Is It WORTH It? Maybe My Child Should Just Get a Job!

At some point in the financial aid application process, you may begin to wonder if it is all worth it. In fact, it's probably safe to say that most families reach a point of at least mild frustration as they gather information about college costs and what their expected contribution will be. It probably doesn't help to continue hearing via the media that college costs in the past decade rose well above the rate of inflation. You may wonder if your child would be better off getting a job now rather than tying up current income and assets (as well as future ones if loans will be part of how you and your child meet college costs).

While each family must develop its own priorities and determine how higher education fits into those priorities, there are some key factors to keep in mind as you make decisions about the value of a college education and the role of finances in your child's decision about where to attend college.

First, there may be some better news in terms of rising college costs. Many experts are convinced that the steep increases in college costs of the 1980s are a thing of the past. Demographics indicate that there will be a significant increase in the number of students of college-going age in the next several years, so colleges may be able to spread out their costs over more students. Colleges are aware of the media, too! The majority of colleges are working to keep their costs down lest parents send their children to less-expensive institutions.

All colleges cost too much.

Actually, very few colleges are truly high-priced. While college costs have risen higher than the inflation rate, college remains accessible and affordable for a majority of Americans. The media has focused attention on the highest-priced colleges (those with tuition and fees over $20,000), to which only about 4 percent of students go, rather than on the 80 percent who attend low-cost community colleges and public four-year colleges. Don't let the misinformation discourage you and your child from the pursuit of higher education!

WHY DO COLLEGES COST WHAT THEY DO?

Each college has its own answer to this question—but there are some common factors that are helpful to understand.

Colleges Are People-Oriented

It's really not possible—or desirable—to make the process of education run like a factory. As you know from your own experience, every student is different, and the teachers who make the most difference in your child's life are the ones who take the time to connect. Highly educated and skilled professors are not an inexpensive commodity, especially in fields like the sciences and engineering, where industry can offer high salaries to draw teachers away. Faculty salaries are a major factor in college costs.

Maintenance and Energy Costs

Consider the costs of maintaining your family dwelling, and multiply exponentially to get some idea of what colleges face. Estimates are staggering for what it would cost to repair and bring into the twenty-first century thousands of campus buildings that were built decades ago. From a cost perspective, consider the energy costs of everything from mini fridges to computer workstations, multiplied by the hundreds or thousands of students and faculty using them on campus.

Technology

Colleges need to cover the costs of providing computer hardware and the networks and mainframes to support them. And then there are the employees who must support the computers and the student and faculty users. In the sciences, there are the additional costs of providing leading-edge research instruments and laboratories. In the arts, even "old technology" can be expensive, given the costs of providing metalworking, enameling, firing, and other specialized facilities.

Declining State Support

Unless your home state enjoys a very high and stable financial base, lawmakers must perform a balancing act every year. State appropriations to education are often an area where cuts are made, or at least increases are not approved. Public colleges depend on the states for the majority of their finances. When budget requests are not approved, tuition increases for in-state and out-of-state students may become a major source of revenue.

Family and Student Expectations

This is not to blame the victim, but it is true that many of the costs associated with higher education have to do with the co-curricular aspects of a college education. For example, students and parents expect top-notch athletic, recreational, and cultural facilities, as well as attractive grounds, varied food service, modern student health facilities, and career placement offices with on-line data bases and staff to provide interview and résumé counseling. Colleges must spend money to upgrade their facilities to attract students to their campuses.

IS COST THE ONLY ISSUE?

If you are certain you will need financial aid to send your child to college, then it would be foolish to suggest that he or she apply only to high-cost institutions or those offering little financial assistance. In fact, every family should consider having at least one "economically safe" college on the list: one where the costs are low and/or the chances for receiving aid, given your child's qualifications, are high. But even this economically safe option should be one your child would be happy to attend if it were the only viable option at the end of the process.

In getting caught up in the financial implications, parents sometimes lose sight of the other factors that might make a particular college a good choice for their child. You don't want your child to end up at a college your family can easily afford but where he or she is unhappy, unchallenged, or unable to pursue a chosen academic major. Many admission officers use the term "fit" to describe the relationship between a student and what a college has to offer. Some of the factors to consider in determining which colleges would be a good "fit" for your child are:

Size

Some students are happiest at smaller colleges where they can get to know most of the other students and the faculty. Others thrive on the variety and energy of a very large university.

Location

Some students will only be happy if they stay close to home, others only if they put some distance between themselves and their home. Some prefer the opportunities afforded by an urban area; others find the bucolic setting of a small-town college more appealing.

Curriculum

It's important to be sure that your child can pursue the major she or he has settled on at this stage—and that there are other options if she or he is like the majority of students who change their major while they are in college.

Other Students

Your child will probably be most comfortable in a setting where he or she is not at the very bottom of the class—or where his or her abilities far outshine those of the majority of students. If your child has special co-curricular interests (sailing, mountain climbing), he or she will be happier in a setting that attracts other students with the same interests.

Job Placement

How likely is the college to support your child in the job search? How successful have alumni been in securing good positions in fields that interest your child?

Graduate School Placement

How likely is the college to prepare your child for graduate school and support his or her application for further study? What percentage of students go on for further study?

You and your child probably considered all or most of these aspects, as well as others, when putting together the college list, but sometimes these important factors are obscured when the financial realities set in. Be sure to keep them in mind when making the final decision about where (or even if) your child attends college. Data continue to support the assumption that the more education, the higher the expected lifetime earnings. You may well find it is worth the financial stretch—or sacrifice—to ensure that your child finds a comfortable environment where he or she will thrive. In the long term, it will be better to have a happy and fulfilled child than a happy and fulfilled checkbook.

WHERE SARAH, JAMES, AND MARIA HAVE DECIDED TO GO AND WHY

SARAH SMITH

Sarah has decided to attend Central, based on qualitative and quantitative considerations. While Old Bricks and Central, her top two choices, both have excellent English programs, Central also has an option to prepare for a career in teaching, should she choose to do so. Central's location in a small town is appealing to Sarah as a change from city life. Sarah also prefers to take on less debt and spend fewer hours at a work-study job her first year in college.

JAMES WASHINGTON

James has decided to enroll at Very Old Bricks, despite having to come up with money to cover the $500 gap left by his aid package and being responsible for larger loan repayments after he graduates. At Very Old Bricks, he will have access to the latest in technology as he prepares for a career in engineering. The college's record in placing students in excellent first jobs and in leading graduate programs also influenced his decision. The campus spirit he felt and the types of students he met when he visited convinced him that Very Old Bricks was the place for him.

MARIA MARTINEZ

Given the fact that she's preparing to face high medical school costs after she completes her undergraduate degree, Maria has decided to attend Canyon.

Her parents have taken out a home equity line of credit to spread out the costs over the academic year. Maria has arranged for on-campus employment in a research lab, where she can earn money and gain experience for medical school. She is excited about the college opportunities that await her at Canyon.

 For more information about college choice:

Admission offices at colleges of interest

College alumni and current students

College and university Web sites

High school guidance counselors

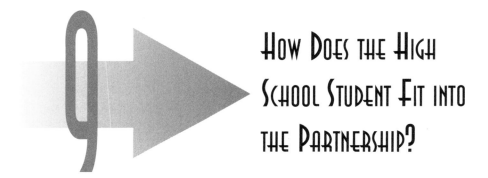

How Does the High School Student Fit into the Partnership?

The preceding chapters have been addressed to your parents, who will probably take the lead in making sure you have the resources you need to attend college. These final two chapters are devoted to you, the student, because you should be aware of specific ways you can participate in the financing of your own education, both while you are still in high school and later as a college student.

WHAT YOU CAN DO WHILE YOU ARE STILL IN HIGH SCHOOL
Ask Questions

Arrange your college visits to allow time to meet with admission and financial aid counselors who can help you and your family answer the "Questions Families Should Ask" presented throughout this book.

Keep Track of Deadlines

Take responsibility for gathering the necessary financial aid application forms and work with your parents to be sure that forms are completed accurately and submitted by the deadlines. Refer often to the worksheet in Chapter 5 to be sure you are taking the right steps at the right time.

Be Ready to Help Financially

Prepare to contribute what is expected of you by the colleges to which you apply. A percentage of your assets, if you have any, will be expected. Many colleges will expect you to contribute a set amount from any job earnings. Keep in mind that if you spend your savings on a car, your investment will depreciate, while your investment in higher education will appreciate!

Learn the Basics of Borrowing

Chances are a loan will be part of the financial aid package offered by one or more of your college choices. Because you'll ultimately be responsible for paying off these debts, it's important to learn how to borrow wisely.

1. Borrow only what you need. You aren't required to borrow the full amount for which you are eligible.

2. Search out lenders with easy application procedures, quick processing and notification, and student services such as toll-free telephone numbers for information and advice.

3. Find a lender that will help you manage your money through repayment options such as graduated repayment (monthly payments begin with a low amount and are adjusted upward as your income increases) or consolidation (combining all your loans into one all-inclusive monthly payment, which lowers the amount of each payment but increases the repayment period).

4. If you elect to take on unsubsidized Federal Stafford or PLUS loans, look for a lender that will allow you to defer principal and interest payments while you are in school.

5. Consider a lender offering one-time capitalization at repayment, which will save you big money when it's time to repay unsubsidized Stafford or PLUS loans. Capitalization, sometimes called compounding, is when a lender accrues interest before the borrower begins to repay the loan; the more frequently interest is capitalized, the more you'll have to pay.

6. Look for a lender with a flexible forbearance policy (temporary postponement of the repayment obligation). If you run into trouble repaying your loan, the lender will be there to help you work out repayment.

7. Look for continuity of servicing. Servicing means processing payments, handling inquiries, and maintaining accurate records. You may well want to avoid a lender that sells loans or contracts services to other organizations, because that can be confusing.

Finish High School on a High Note

You'll face lots of distractions as you wind up your high school career: co-curricular and social activities, the whole admission and financial aid application process, and other obligations. In the midst of all this, don't forget to keep up with your academics. Not only will a strong high school record enable you to hit the ground running when you start college, but it may help you qualify for the type of financial aid colleges award to their preferred candidates. So keep up the good work!

 For more information on student financing options:

Admission and financial aid offices at colleges of interest

College and university Web sites

College Blue Book: Scholarships, Fellowships, Grants and Loans. 25th ed. New York: Macmillan Publishing Co., 1993. Lists sources of financial aid assistance for high school seniors through students in advanced professional programs.

College Board Online: *www.collegeboard.org*

ExPAN

College Costs and Financial Aid Handbook, 1998

College Board Scholarship Handbook

High school guidance counselors

Need a Lift? Educational Opportunities, Careers, Loans, Scholarships, Employment. 46th ed. Indianapolis: The American Legion Education Program. Updated annually. Sources of career, scholarship, and loan information for all students, with emphasis on scholarships for veterans, their dependents, and children of deceased or disabled veterans.

The Student Guide. Washington, D.C.: U.S. Department of Education, Office of Student Financial Assistance. Detailed information on federal student aid programs, eligibility rules, application procedures. Free. Order from Federal Student Aid Programs, P.O. Box 84, Washington, D.C. 20044, or call 1-800-433-3243.

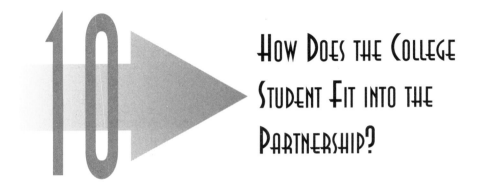

How Does the College Student Fit into the Partnership?

Once you are in college, you'll have plenty to keep you busy, academically and socially. The challenges of applying for admission and first-year financial aid will be replaced by new challenges. Yet you'll want to keep on top of your finances throughout college, not only to ensure that you can continue to pay for college but also to ensure that you begin your post-college years on as firm a financial footing as possible.

MANAGING YOUR MONEY RESPONSIBLY
Develop a Budget

A simple budget plan will help you avoid problems like running out of money before the semester is over. Write down all your financial obligations in one column and the funds or income that will cover those obligations in another. Think about the way you'll spend your money each month during the school year. Then, write out your budget plan, consult it often, and stick to it! The worksheet at the end of this chapter will help you get started.

Open a Checking Account

A checking account will help you keep track of where your money goes. Always keep enough money in your checking account to cover the checks you write. Record all your deposits, withdrawals, and checks in your checkbook register; balance your checkbook every month. Hold onto your canceled checks, because they provide a record of your spending and serve as proof that you paid for something.

Beware of the ATM

Many banks have Automated Teller Machines, which can be a real convenience if you need cash after regular banking hours or when you're too busy to get to the bank. But they can also be the fast track to financial problems, because it's so easy to withdraw money. Try not to visit the ATM too often. When you do make withdrawals, you'll waste less money if you take out smaller amounts. Save your ATM receipts and be sure to record them in your checkbook register.

Say "No" to Credit Cards

Credit cards are a great way to get into financial trouble. Banks are happy to offer you a credit card; but beware, these cards are really loans in disguise because the bank charges you interest if you don't pay the whole bill at the end of the month. When you use your credit card, you must make a monthly payment that includes interest or finance charges of up to 23 percent until the total bill is paid off. You may also have to pay an annual fee of $20 or more just for use of the card. You could pay even more if you use your card to get a cash advance (a very bad idea). If you feel you must have a credit card, save it for a real money emergency.

Pay Bills on Time

If you can't pay the whole amount you owe, pay the minimum allowed on the bill. By making at least the minimum payment each month, you'll have a clean payment record and build a good credit rating for the future.

Reduce Your Costs

Write letters or send e-mail instead of calling long-distance. Buy used books instead of new ones, or pool resources with friends and share books. Save more money by reading library copies of some of the books on your list. Compare residence hall costs with those of apartment living. Some students can save substantial amounts by living off campus and sharing the costs of rent and utilities. (Of course, this works only if you avoid high-rent districts and find good roommates.) Or you may be in a situation where continuing to live at home makes sense. No matter where you live, you can make your money go further by fixing some of your own meals and taking advantage of free campus entertainment.

Accelerate Your Degree

This isn't an option for everyone, but if you come into college with some credits earned in high school, or take college courses in the summer, you may be able to graduate a semester or more early, thus saving tuition and living expenses.

FINANCIAL AID RENEWAL
Keep Your Grades Up

Many grant and loan programs, including those administered through the federal government, require that you maintain a certain grade-point average (GPA) and make satisfactory progress toward a degree in order to qualify for renewal of aid.

Learn Your College's Renewal Policies

If you haven't already checked with your college's financial aid office about their aid renewal policies, be sure to do so in the first semester. You'll want to be sure to have the required forms on hand.

Be Timely and Accurate When You Renew Your Application

Be aware of the deadlines for applying for aid renewal, and work with your parents to be sure forms are completed accurately and submitted on time.

Borrow Responsibly

Borrow only what you need. Being eligible to borrow doesn't mean you have to take the maximum the lender will allow. Remember, you're expected to repay your loans, plus interest. Repaying your loans on time will help you establish a good credit rating—very important when it's time to find a job, rent an apartment, or buy a car.

YOUR CREDIT HISTORY AND PROFESSIONAL SCHOOL

If you're planning to apply for admission to professional school, it's likely you'll need to borrow money to continue your education. But did you know that your admission may be dependent on your ability to demonstrate clean credit? You'll need a credit history, in the form of a credit report, that shows you've been responsible in paying back your debts.

Most professional schools will require a copy of your credit report after you've been accepted for admission, but before you've been offered a financial aid package. If your credit report shows a number of late or missed payments on your credit cards or car loan, for example, or charging over your credit limit, you could be denied admission or an alternative loan for graduate school.

The following are answers to questions regarding credit reports and how to get a negative credit history back on track without jeopardizing your education.

When should I get a copy of my credit report?

Send for it well before you apply to graduate or professional school. This will give you time to review your credit history and resolve problems or errors you may find in your report. Ask your financial aid office which credit reporting agency they use, then contact that agency to request a copy of your report. There are three major reporting agencies—Experian, Trans Union, and Equifax—and each could have its own file on you. If you plan to apply for a College Board sponsored CollegeCredit loan, call Experian first at 1-800-392-1122 for recorded instructions. If they do not have a file on you, call Trans Union at 1-216-779-7200, and then Equifax at 1-800-685-1111. To view a sample credit report on the Internet, go to: *http://www.experian.com/personal/sample.html.*

What should I do when I receive my credit report?

Check the report carefully for errors. Make sure the reporting agency hasn't confused you with someone else with the same name or a similar social security number, and that they haven't included incorrect information about you and your accounts. If you find a mistake or have questions about your report, follow the instructions included in the report. If you do not receive a reply within 30 days, call the credit reporting agency.

What if I disagree with information in my credit report?

For those items in your credit report that you disagree with, such as a credit card account that was paid late due to unexpected medical bills or another real financial emergency, send a brief statement to the credit reporting agency. The information you provide will be placed on your credit profile and will be included each time your report is accessed.

What if my credit report shows one or more 90-day delinquencies or my school or lender determines I have a negative credit history?

You may still be able to borrow if you can document extenuating circumstances. Your documentation may include, but is not limited to:

➡ An updated credit report that shows you are no longer 90 or more days delinquent on a debt. You may also use an updated report to correct other information on the original credit report that resulted in the adverse ruling.

➡ A statement from your creditors that you have made satisfactory arrangements to repay the debt or debts that are the basis for the adverse credit ruling.

➡ In the case of a debt with an outstanding balance that is less than $500 but is 90 or more days delinquent, you may provide, in writing, a satisfactory explanation for the delinquency.

I have late payments on my credit report, and I don't want potential lenders or employers to see them. Should I use one of those companies that claim they can get this kind of information removed from my credit report?

No. Companies that say they can "fix" your credit profile are usually scams that take your money. There is nothing they can do for you that you cannot do for yourself. Accurate information remains part of your credit history, whether positive or not. Only time will fix "bad" credit.

How long does negative credit information remain in my file?

Credit and collection accounts and court records, such as judgments, remain on file for seven years (five years in New York) from the date of last activity. It's important to remember that even if you paid your account in full, the negative information will not be removed from your credit file until the required years have passed. However, the account will appear as paid on your report.

Can I rebuild my credit history?

Yes. The good news is, your credit report is continually evolving. When you use credit responsibly and pay your bills on time, you're building a positive credit history. When a lender or credit card issuer considers your application, it often pays much more attention to your bill-paying pattern during the most recent two years than to your record of five years ago or longer. The negative information on your report should not prevent you from borrowing in the future if you can demonstrate that you are a good credit risk by paying your bills on time over a period of 18 to 24 months.

Where can I get help in managing my debts?

If you're finding it difficult to pay your bills, the nonprofit National Foundation for Consumer Credit has member agencies that can help you establish a budget and negotiate a repayment plan with your creditors. Call 1-800-388-2227 for the location of an agency near you.

For more information on responsible student financing:

College financial aid office

College Web site

College Board Online: *www.collegeboard.org*

The Student Guide

Questions Students Should Ask the College About the
Financial Aid Reapplication Process

1. What financial aid forms are required for aid renewal?

2. When are the forms due to be completed and returned to the processor and/or college?

3. Will renewal of financial aid be dependent on my academic
   progress? What are the guidelines for maintaining satisfactory
   academic progress?

4. Will a copy of my parents' completed tax forms be required? If so,
   when?

5. When will I receive notification of my financial aid package?

6. What is the deadline for accepting the financial aid offer?

$ WORKSHEET 8: BUDGETING FOR THE SEMESTER

Estimated Expenses for Semester

Tuition	$ _____
Fees	_____
Books/Supplies	_____
Rent/Housing	_____
Board/Meals	_____
Phone/Utilities	_____
Clothing	_____
Laundry/Dry Cleaning	_____
Transportation	
(carfare, gas, parking,	
insurance, etc.)	_____
Medical/Dental	_____
Recreation	_____
Personal Expenses	_____
Savings	_____
Child Care	_____
Credit Card Debt	_____
Other	_____
TOTAL SEMESTER EXPENSES	$ _____

Projected Income for Semester

Money from Parents	$ _____
Money from Savings	_____
Work/Study	_____
Other Work	_____
Scholarships	_____
Grants	_____
Loans	_____
Public Benefits	
(Social Security,	
Veterans Admin., etc.)	_____
Spouse's Wages	_____
Other	_____
TOTAL SEMESTER INCOME	$ _____

NOTE: If your total semester expenses exceed your total semester income, carefully review your spending habits and look for areas where you can economize.

WORKSHEET 9: TRACKING FINANCIAL AID RENEWAL REQUIREMENTS

Use this worksheet to keep track of deadlines for renewing your financial aid award. Your financial aid administrator will provide you with renewal requirements.

Forms	Required?	Due Date	Date Completed
Renewal FAFSA			
CSS PROFILE			
• Registration			
• Application			
College Application			
Tax Forms			
Other:			

Glossary

Candidate's Reply Date Agreement: Colleges adhering to this agreement will not require admitted freshman applicants to notify the college of their decision to attend, or to accept an offer of financial aid, before May 1. The purpose of the agreement is to give applicants time to hear from all the colleges to which they applied before having to make a commitment to any one of them.

Capitalization: When a lender accrues interest before the borrower begins repayment, then adds that amount to the principal. Sometimes also called "compounding." Capitalizing increases the total to be repaid and the size of the minimum monthly payment. Students can avoid capitalizing interest by paying the accrued interest. Lenders may capitalize no more frequently than quarterly; the more frequently interest is capitalized, the higher the interest payments.

CollegeCredit: An educational loan program sponsored by the College Board that offers a convenient, single source for multiple financing options for students and parents.

College Scholarship Service (CSS): The financial aid division of the College Board that provides a variety of information, application, and processing services to students and parents, secondary schools, and colleges and universities.

Consolidation: Combining two or more loans into one new loan that has a longer repayment term and a single monthly payment that is smaller than the sum of previous monthly payments. By consolidating eligible federal student loans and extending the repayment term (up to 30 years, depending on the total loan amount), repayment can be easier. Note that while this may ease the borrower's cash flow, consolidation can add significantly to the amount of overall interest that is paid over time.

Cooperative education: Also called "co-op education," this is a program in which students alternate between periods of full-time study and full-time paid employment, usually in a related field. Typically five years are required to complete a bachelor's degree in a cooperative education program. Some colleges refer to this as "work-study," but it should not be confused with the Federal Work-Study Program.

CSS/Financial Aid PROFILE: A data collection and need analysis service required by many colleges, universities, and private scholarship programs in addition to the FAFSA. PROFILE is used in awarding private financial aid funds. Students pay a fee to register for PROFILE and have reports sent to institutions and programs that use it.

Cost of Attendance: This figure is determined for each college by totaling the costs for tuition and fees, room and board, fees, books and supplies, personal expenses, and travel.

Early Decision/Early Action: These admission programs are offered at some colleges for students who have determined that the college is their first choice. Early Decision candidates must attend the college if they are admitted under the program; Early Action candidates simply hear earlier than other students what the decision is but are not required to attend if admitted. Students may pick only one college to which to apply under an Early Decision program.

Family Contribution: The total amount a student and his or her family are expected to pay toward college costs from their income and assets. The amount is derived from a need analysis of a family's overall financial circumstances. Federal Methodology is used in determining a student's eligibility for federal, and in most cases state-funded, student aid. Some colleges and private aid programs may use a different methodology (Institutional Methodology or some derivative of it) in determining eligibility for nonfederal sources of financial aid.

Federal Direct Loan Program: Students at participating colleges can borrow subsidized or unsubsidized Federal Direct Loans through this college-administered program. The federal government pays the interest on subsidized direct loans while students are enrolled in college at least half time, if the loan is based on demonstrated need. For unsubsidized loans, students will usually be asked to make interest payments while enrolled in school. Following a six-month grace period after graduating from or leaving school, all students borrowing in the Federal Direct Loan Program must begin repaying principal and interest.

Federal PLUS Loans: This program permits parents of dependent undergraduate students to borrow up to the full cost of education minus any other financial aid the student may have received. To be eligible, parents must usually pass a credit check.

Federal Pell Grant Program: A federally sponsored and administered program that provides grants based on exceptional need to undergraduate students. Congress annually sets the dollar range for grants.

Federal Perkins Loan Program: A federally funded program based on exceptional need, administered by colleges, that provides low-interest loans for undergraduate and graduate students. Repayment does not begin until nine months after the student graduates from or leaves college.

Federal Stafford Loan Program: A federal program that allows students to borrow to meet educational expenses. Funds are borrowed directly from banks or other lending institutions. The federal government pays the interest on subsidized Stafford loans while students are enrolled in college at least half time, if the loan is based on demonstrated need. For unsubsidized loans, students may be asked to make interest payments while enrolled in school. Following a six-month grace period after graduating from or leaving school, all students borrowing in the Federal Stafford Loan Program must begin repaying principal and interest.

Federal Supplemental Educational Opportunity Grant Program: A federal program administered by colleges to provide grant aid to undergraduate students with exceptional financial need.

Federal Work-Study (FWS): A federally sponsored, campus-based program. Participating colleges provide employment opportunities for students with demonstrated need who are enrolled for undergraduate or graduate study. In assigning work to aid recipients, colleges take into account the recipient's skills, class schedule, academic progress, and interest in community service.

Financial Aid Award Letter: A notice from a college or other financial aid sponsor that tells the student how much aid is being offered. The award letter also usually explains how a student's financial need was determined, describes the contents of the financial aid package, and outlines any conditions attached to the award.

Financial Aid Package: The total financial aid award received by the student. It may be made up of a combination or "package" of aid that includes both gift aid and self-help. Many colleges try to meet a student's full financial need, but availability of funds, institutional aid policies, and the number of students needing assistance all influence the composition of a financial aid package.

Financial Need: The amount by which a student's family contribution falls short of covering the cost of attendance. Assessments of need may differ depending on the need analysis methodology used.

Forbearance: An authorized period of time during which the lender agrees to temporarily postpone a borrower's total loan repayment obligation. At the borrower's request, an extension of time or smaller monthly payments may be authorized. Forbearance is granted at the lender's discretion when a borrower demonstrates good intentions of repaying but is temporarily unable to do so. A borrower must request forbearance from the lender. Forbearance does not alter the repayment status of the loan and interest continues to accrue.

Free Application for Federal Student Aid (FAFSA): A form distributed and processed by the United States Department of Education, used in applying for all Federal Title IV student aid programs, including Pell Grants, Stafford

Loans, and campus-based programs (SEOG, Work-Study, and Perkins Loans). The FAFSA collects information required to determine eligibility according to the Federal Methodology. In many states, completion of the FAFSA is also sufficient to establish eligibility for state-sponsored aid programs. Forms are widely available in high schools and colleges, and may be filed anytime after January 1 of the year for which a student is seeking aid.

Gift Aid: Student financial aid, such as scholarships and grants, that does not have to be repaid and does not require a student's being employed.

Interest: The fee charged a borrower for the use of someone else's money, computed as a percentage of what is borrowed. The interest rate may remain constant throughout the life of the loan (i.e., fixed) or may change at specified times (i.e., variable).

Lender: A financial institution such as a bank, savings and loan association, a credit union, or qualified program (i.e., the College Board's CollegeCredit Program) that makes Federal Family Education and PLUS loans, as well as other private loans, to students and parents.

Need Analysis: The process by which a financial aid sponsor determines a family's demonstrated need for financial assistance. Demonstrated need is determined to be the difference between what a family can afford (the family contribution) and the cost of attendance at each college to which the student applies. Differences in calculation of need arise from a variety of factors, including the methodology used to determine the family contribution and the varying costs of colleges.

Parent Contribution: The amount a student's parents are expected to pay toward college costs from their income and assets. The amount is derived from need analysis of the parents' overall financial situation. The parent contribution and the student contribution together constitute the total family contribution that, when subtracted from the cost of attendance, equals financial need. Generally, students are eligible for financial aid up to their financial need.

Satisfactory Academic Progress: Many financial aid sponsors require that students make satisfactory progress to continue to qualify for aid. To receive federal student aid, students must maintain satisfactory academic progress toward completion of a degree or certificate each term. All colleges have a statement defining the required level of progress. Some colleges have additional academic standards for renewal of institutionally sponsored awards.

Self-Help: Student financial aid, such as loans and jobs, that requires repayment or a student's being employed.

Student Aid Report (SAR): A report produced by the U.S. Department of Education and sent to students who have applied for federal financial aid. The SAR information is used by colleges to determine eligibility for Federal Pell Grants and other federal financial aid programs such as the Federal Work-Study Program, Federal Perkins Loan Program, Federal Supplemental Educational Opportunity Grants, Federal Family Education Loan Program, and the Federal Direct Loan Program.

Student Contribution: The amount students are expected to pay from their income, assets, and benefits toward college costs. The amount is derived from a need analysis of the student's resources. The student contribution and the parent contribution constitute the total family contribution that, when subtracted from the student budget, equals financial need. Generally, students are eligible for financial aid up to their financial need.

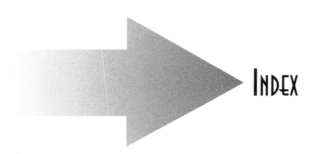

Index

About the Author

Deb Thyng Schmidt graduated from Bates College in 1977 summa cum laude and Phi Beta Kappa, and earned a master's degree in English from the University of Wisconsin-Madison in 1980. Her career has been spent in education, mainly in the area of college admission. At Carleton College, she directed the alumni admission volunteers program; at Cornell University, she was responsible for the development and coordination of university-wide undergraduate admission and financial aid communications. Since moving to Colorado in 1995, she has worked as a freelance writer for a number of institutions and organizations, including the College Scholarship Service, Cornell University, The Dawson School, and Marywood College. She also serves as a trustee of Bates College.